PIZZA PRESTO

PIZZA PRESTO

80 Fast & Fabulous Recipes

Norman Kolpas

CONTEMPORARY BOOKS

A TRIBUNE COMPANY

Library of Congress Cataloging-in-Publication Data

Kolpas, Norman.
     Pizza presto : 80 fast & fabulous recipes / Norman Kolpas.
       p.   cm.
  Includes index.
  ISBN 0-8092-3220-0
  1. Pizza. 2. Quick and easy cookery.   I. Title.
TX770.P58K654   1996
641.8'24—dc20   96-11466
                                                CIP

Featured on the cover: Shrimp with Roasted Peppers,
   Pine Nuts, and Pesto (see page 56)

Cover design by Kim Bartko
Cover photograph by Chris Cassidy
Foodstyling by Kim Loughlin
Interior design by Nancy Freeborn

Published by Contemporary Books, Inc.
Two Prudential Plaza, Chicago, Illinois 60601-6790
Manufactured in the United States of America
International Standard Book Number: 0-8092-3220-0
10   9   8   7   6   5   4   3   2   1

For Katie and Jacob

Contents

Preface

Over the past decade a quiet revolution has changed the way millions of Americans enjoy their favorite food, pizza. Prebaked pizza crusts marketed nationwide make it possible to prepare and enjoy a freshly made pizza at home in a matter of minutes. Widely sold premade sauces and a host of ready-to-add toppings make it all the easier.

Yet many home cooks are confounded instead of delighted by these revolutionary products. You smear on some pizza sauce and sprinkle on some mozzarella; or you follow the few recipes on the backs of the packages. "Then what?" you ask yourself. "What can I do that's as exciting and original as the wide array of pizzas I see nowadays on the menus of Italian trattorias and other restaurants?"

Pizza Presto offers you an answer 80 times over, with recipes to put fresh-baked pizza on your table in next to no time—many in less than 15 minutes!

In the first chapter, you'll find a discussion of basic ingredients and how to shop for them. I urge you to read this chapter carefully, especially since I've kept it brief. (The point of this book, after all, is *speed.*) I've even included a couple of easy recipes to make your own pizza sauces if you can't find them premade in your market, along with instructions for roasting peppers and garlic. Chapter 2 provides some very basic instructions on making pizzas using prebaked crusts.

The recipe chapters are divided by featured ingredients: Meat and Poultry, Seafood, Vegetables, and Cheese and Eggs. You'll notice that each recipe includes *two* sets of quantities—one for a 6-inch prebaked crust that serves one, the other for a large 12-inch crust that can serve four to six people. When following these recipes feel free to vary the amounts and ingredients to suit your own tastes and inspirations; the point of any cooking, after all, is to have fun and give pleasure to yourself and others.

Acknowledgments

As always, my friends at Contemporary Books have been exemplary in their encouragement and support. Nancy Crossman is always a pleasure to work with. Gerilee Hundt unflappably looks after manuscripts. And Kim Bartko, Tina Chapman, Alina Cowden, Gigi Grajdura, Maureen Musker, Audrey Sails, Terry Stone, and Kathy Willhoite have each in his or her way played a part in making this a better project. Thanks also to photographer Chris Cassidy and stylist Kim Loughlin for their lovely cover image.

CHAPTER ONE

The Pizza Presto Pantry

The main point this book aims to make is that, at its simplest, preparing a pizza with a prebaked pizza crust involves little more cooking expertise than knowing how to turn on your oven.

By shopping wisely in a well-stocked supermarket, you can pick up already prepared ingredients that you can arrange atop a prebaked pizza crust without even having to pick up a knife. Admittedly, a handful of the recipes in this book do call for some very quick sautéing, grilling, or simmering of ingredients before you place them on the pizza; but even these make use of convenient ingredients.

The following guide reviews the ingredients used most frequently in this book.

Prebaked Pizza Crusts

You'll find these in see-through plastic wrappers hanging near the dairy case or in the bread section of most well-stocked supermarkets. The most common brand, and the one that really started the craze for these exceptionally convenient food items, is Boboli®, but other manufacturers are jumping on the bandwagon as well.

Their dough already lightly flavored with olive oil, garlic, and cheese and baked to a golden brown, these crusts are delicious in their own right. But add a sauce, toppings, and cheese, and bake in the oven long enough to melt the cheese and crisp up the bread, and you have something that comes mighty close to a fresh-baked pizza.

Prebaked pizza crusts are commonly available in small sizes measuring about 6 inches in diameter—a perfect single serving—and large sizes about 12 inches in diameter, generous enough to serve four to six people. For this reason, I've included two sets of ingredient measurements for every recipe in this book. The first set is for the small crusts; the other is for the large.

Prebaked pizza crusts are perishable. Their packaging is stamped with a sell-by date, to which you should pay careful attention before purchasing. Store at cool room temperature in the unopened package and use within five days of purchase; or freeze in the package for a month or longer.

Sauces

Manufacturers of prebaked pizza crusts have begun to market ready-to-use pizza sauces. Well-made and well-seasoned, these products work very well.

But you don't have to limit your search for sauce to the prebaked pizza crust display. Scan the refrigerator case of a well-stocked supermarket and you'll find still more sauces—marinara, tomato-basil, various pestos, cheese-and-cream mixtures—that can be used for any of the recipes in this book or for your own creations.

As you scan the recipes, you'll also see that I make occasional use of other sauces as well. Heavy cream, French-style crème fraîche, or Italian mascarpone moisten and enrich the crust. Mustard, on its own or blended with some cream, can enliven a pizza just as it does a sandwich. Then there are the fresh Mexican tomato salsas, bottled barbecue sauces, and Chinese hoisin sauce. Almost every aisle of the market seems to yield another option. Some pizzas call for cheese alone. I urge you to explore the many options open to you. And should you wish to make your own simple sauce, here are two classic recipes:

Pizza Sauce

MAKES ABOUT 2 CUPS

A simple, all-purpose tomato-based pizza sauce. Store extra sauce covered in the refrigerator for up to 1 week or in a freezer container for 2 to 3 months.

> *2 tablespoons extra-virgin olive oil*
>
> *2 garlic cloves, chopped fine*
>
> *2 shallots or ½ small onion, chopped fine*
>
> *1 28-ounce can crushed tomatoes*
>
> *1 tablespoon sugar*
>
> *½ tablespoon dried oregano, crumbled*
>
> *½ tablespoon dried basil, crumbled*
>
> *¾ teaspoon salt*
>
> *2 bay leaves*

In a medium saucepan, heat the olive oil over medium heat. Add the garlic and shallots or onion and sauté until transparent, 3 to 5 minutes. Stir in the remaining ingredients, reduce the heat to medium-low and simmer, stirring frequently, until thick, about 30 minutes.

Pesto Sauce

MAKES ABOUT 1 CUP

A classic of Genoa, Italy, this sauce has many variations. Add more or less garlic to suit your taste. If the basil tastes too strong for you, replace part of it with parsley. If you have any left over, put it in a small glass or plastic container, smooth its surface, and pour a thin film of olive oil on top to cover; then cover the container with a lid or plastic wrap and refrigerate for 3 to 5 days. Stir in the oil before use.

1 cup packed fresh basil leaves
½ cup freshly grated Parmesan cheese
½ cup extra-virgin olive oil
⅓ cup shelled pine nuts
2 medium garlic cloves, peeled

Put all the ingredients in a food processor fitted with the metal blade. Pulse the machine on and off to chop them coarsely, then scrape down the bowl. Process continuously, stopping once or twice to scrape down the bowl, until the pesto is smooth.

Fresh Vegetables

Your supermarket's produce section, or your local greengrocer, is an outstanding source for quick pizza toppings. Many vegetables—chief among them mushrooms, onions, and peppers—need only to be sliced thinly and then strewn on top of the sauce. Others might benefit from slight precooking—grilling eggplant, for example, or parboiling asparagus. If you're especially pressed for time, you might also check to see if your supermarket has caught on to the trend of prepackaged ready-cut vegetables, or of a salad bar offering a wide variety of prepared items that you need only take out of the package and strew across a pizza.

Fresh Herbs

Garnishes of four commonly available fresh herbs—parsley, basil, chives, and cilantro—add extra spark to many of the quick pizzas in this book. If you can't find them and are pressed for time, however, you can omit this final flourish.

Preserved Vegetables

The canned goods or pickles and preserves sections of your supermarket offer still more options for embellishing a quick pizza. Marinated artichoke hearts, roasted bell peppers packed in oil, brine-packed or marinated hearts of palm, oil-packed sun-dried tomatoes, marinated olives of every description—any of these can be used individually or in combination to make a memorable pizza. If your market's supply is limited, seek out an Italian delicatessen, which is likely to offer a broad array of imported items.

Roasting Bell Peppers

Though store-bought already-roasted peppers are exceptionally convenient, it is easy to roast raw bell peppers yourself whenever you need them. To roast peppers, place them on a foil-lined baking sheet in a 450°F oven. Roast until evenly blistered and browned, 15 to 25 minutes depending on the size. Turn the peppers several times to promote even roasting. Remove from the oven and cover with a kitchen towel until cool enough to handle. Pull out the stems of the cooled peppers and peel away their blackened skins. Then open up the peppers and remove their seeds, using a small spoon to pick up any strays.

Roasting Garlic Cloves

Though you may find already-roasted garlic for sale in some upscale markets and delis, it is easy to roast it at home for yourself. Wrap a whole head of garlic, its individual cloves unseparated, in heavy-duty aluminum foil or a double thickness of regular foil. Roast in a 425°F oven until the cloves are soft enough to be pierced with no resistance by the tip of a small sharp knife—about 1 hour. Remove from the oven and leave the garlic to cool in its foil. Carefully separate the cloves and squeeze them from their skins, one by one, into a small bowl filled with olive oil. Make sure the garlic is completely submerged; then cover the bowl with plastic wrap and refrigerate.

Meats, Poultry, and Seafood

Many well-stocked markets carry a wide variety of cooked meat, poultry, and seafood products. There are all kinds of deli meats and sausages, barbecued or smoked chicken, roast turkey breast, cooked crabmeat and shrimp, smoked salmon, and so on. Each of these items makes a great addition to a quick pizza. For other options, look for items that you can cook quickly before adding them to the pizza, such as ground meat or poultry, all kinds of fresh sausages, or fresh shrimp. Don't ignore canned goods either. Canned tuna and anchovies, in particular, are excellent pizza toppings.

Cheeses

For many people, *cheese* and *pizza* are synonymous. The pizzas in this book make use of a wide variety of cheeses. Some are prized for their melting quality, such as mozzarella and fontina. Some add special flavor or tang, such as Parmesan, feta, or the various kinds of blue cheese. Some are prized for their soft, moist texture, like ricotta. Still others contribute a number of different characteristics, most notably creamy, tangy, smooth, fresh goat cheese. Quick pizzas are made all the easier by the many prepackaged shredded cheeses you'll find in your supermarket dairy case. Bear in mind, however, that you'll be paying extra for this processing, and that it takes little extra effort or time on your part to simply grate the cheese yourself. Feel free, as well, to substitute your own favorite cheeses—or whatever is available at a moment's notice—for those called for in the recipes in this book.

CHAPTER TWO

Making Pizza Presto

There is so little effort involved in making a pizza with a prebaked crust that you really need no more instructions than you'll find in any one of the recipes in this book. Nevertheless, these few basic pieces of information will make the task even more streamlined.

Preheating the Oven

In every recipe, the oven is preheated to 450°F, the optimum temperature for heating and crisping the crust in the same time it takes for a cheese topping to melt. Note, too, that none of the recipes calls for using a pizza brick or baking stone. If you have one, however, you can keep it in the oven and use a pizza paddle or rimless baking sheet to slide the pizza onto it; the stone will contribute to a slightly crisper crust, and may reduce baking time by a minute or so.

The Baking Sheet

Before placing any sauce or topping on the pizza crust, always put it on a sturdy baking sheet. This will facilitate putting it into and taking it out of the oven without losing any of its toppings.

Spreading Sauce and Arranging Toppings

Note that all recipes call for you to leave an uncovered area ½-inch wide around the rim of the pizza. This will help prevent sauce and toppings from overflowing and provide you with a neat edge with which to hold individual slices should you wish to eat them by hand.

Baking the Pizza

Baking times are listed as about 10 minutes. But this may vary with your individual oven, as well as with how browned you want the cheese on your pizza, so keep a careful watch, starting to check after about 8 minutes.

Cutting the Pizza

The rolling wheel-type pizza cutter traditionally used in pizzerias can tend to drag ingredients messily across the pizza's surface. There are two ways to avoid this. If you use the wheel, start by pressing it down firmly in the center of the pizza for each cut, rolling it toward the rim. An even better method, I find, is to use a large chef's knife or cleaver to cut the pizza, pressing it straight down through cheese, toppings, and crust.

Eating the Pizza

While the recipes in this book call for cutting the pizzas into serving slices, bear in mind that the more toppings there are on a pizza, the harder it will be for you to eat those slices by hand. Make sure you and your guests are armed with knives and forks when you serve the pizza.

CHAPTER THREE

Meat and Poultry Toppings

Sausage, Roasted Peppers, and Pesto

Chunky Pepperoni with Diced Mozzarella

Prosciutto and Mushroom

Radicchio and Prosciutto

Garlic Salami with Ricotta

Italian BLT

Mexicana with Chorizo and Chilies

Hawaiian-Style with Ham, Pineapple, and Monterey Jack

Sloppy Joes

Ground Beef and Onion

Picadillo-Style Ground Beef

Moroccan Lamb

The Ultimate Barbecued Chicken with Roasted Peppers, Sweet Onion, and Smoked Cheeses

Seared Chicken with Sautéed Leeks and Dolcelatte

Chicken Fajitas

Smoked Chicken with Pesto, Red Onions, and Provolone

Ham and Aged Provolone with Mustard Cream

Chinese Minced Chicken

Southwestern Turkey

Day-After-Thanksgiving Pizza

Monte Cristo with Turkey, Ham, Provolone, and Dijon Cream

Sausage, Roasted Peppers, and Pesto

MAKES 1 6-INCH PIZZA *(serves 1) or* 1 12-INCH PIZZA *(serves 4–6)*

This pizza finds its inspiration in the classic Italian sandwich filling of sausage and peppers. Seek out one of the outstanding quality fresh sausages now widely available, whether made from pork, beef, chicken, turkey, or even lamb. Using preroasted bottled peppers makes the recipe all the easier. You can substitute pizza sauce for the pesto, if you like.

Prebaked pizza crust	*6-inch*	*12-inch*
Sweet or spicy fresh Italian sausage,		
about 4 ounces	*1*	*4*
Pesto sauce	*3 tablespoons*	*¾ cup*
Roasted red bell pepper	*½*	*2*
Shredded fontina cheese	*1½ ounces*	*6 ounces*
Shredded mozzarella cheese	*1½ ounces*	*6 ounces*

Preheat the oven to 450°F. Place the pizza crust on a baking sheet.

Put the sausage in a saucepan and add enough cold water to cover. Bring to a boil over medium heat, draining off the water as soon as it reaches a full boil.

With a fork, puncture the sausage two or three times. Heat a nonstick frying pan over medium heat, add the sausage and sear until lightly browned on all sides, 3 to 4 minutes. Remove from the pan and cut into ¼-inch-thick slices.

Spread the pesto on top of the pizza crust up to ½ inch from its edge. Arrange the sausage slices on top of the pizza, pressing them into the sauce. Tear the roasted pepper into thin strips and scatter them on top, then sprinkle evenly with the fontina and mozzarella cheeses.

Bake the pizza until the cheese has melted and begun to brown lightly, about 10 minutes. Remove from the oven, transfer to a cutting board, and cut into slices.

Chunky Pepperoni with Diced Mozzarella

MAKES 1 6-INCH PIZZA (*serves 1*) *or* 1 12-INCH PIZZA (*serves 4–6*)

Whenever I've eaten pepperoni pizza, I've always been slightly irked by the way a piece of the spicy sausage will invariably pull off half the topping when I bite into it. The solution is obvious: cut the pepperoni into bite-sized chunks, whether you buy it already sliced or as a whole sausage.

Prebaked pizza crust	6-inch	12-inch
Pizza sauce	3 tablespoons	¾ cup
Freshly grated Parmesan cheese	1 tablespoon	¼ cup
Pepperoni sausage, cut into		
½-inch pieces	3 ounces	¾ pound
Shredded mozzarella cheese	1 ounce	¼ pound
Dried oregano	¼ teaspoon	1 teaspoon

Preheat the oven to 450°F. Place the pizza crust on a baking sheet.

Spread the pizza sauce on top of the crust up to ½ inch from its edge. Sprinkle the Parmesan evenly over the sauce. Scatter the pepperoni chunks on top. Finish with a layer of mozzarella. With your fingertips, crumble the oregano evenly over the cheese.

Bake the pizza until the cheese is bubbly and just beginning to brown, about 10 minutes. Remove from the oven, transfer to a cutting board, and cut into slices.

Prosciutto and Mushroom

MAKES 1 6-INCH PIZZA (*serves 1*) *or* 1 12-INCH PIZZA (*serves 4–6*)

Placing the prosciutto on top of the cheese allows it to frizzle a bit in the oven's heat, developing its flavor and texture all the more appealingly. This topping is also excellent with pesto sauce. If you like goat cheese or garlic-herb cream cheese, dot a little over the mushrooms before topping with the other cheese.

Prebaked pizza crust	*6-inch*	*12-inch*
Pizza sauce	*3 tablespoons*	*¾ cup*
Freshly grated Parmesan cheese	*1 tablespoon*	*¼ cup*
Medium-sized cultivated mushrooms, sliced thick	*3*	*12*
Shredded mozzarella cheese	*3 ounces*	*¾ pound*
Freshly ground black pepper to taste		
Prosciutto, sliced thin	*1 ounce*	*¼ pound*
Fresh basil, shredded fine	*½ tablespoon*	*2 tablespoons*

Preheat the oven to 450°F. Place the pizza crust on a baking sheet.

Spread the pizza sauce on top of the crust up to ½ inch from its edge. Sprinkle evenly with the Parmesan and arrange the mushrooms on top. Spread the mozzarella evenly over the mushrooms, sprinkle lightly with the black pepper, and then drape the prosciutto over the cheese.

Bake the pizza until the cheese has melted, about 10 minutes. Remove from the oven, transfer to a cutting board, garnish with basil, and cut into slices.

Radicchio and Prosciutto

MAKES 1 6-INCH PIZZA (*serves 1*) *or* 1 12-INCH PIZZA (*serves 4–6*)

Small purplish-red heads of radicchio have a refreshing crispness coupled with a pleasant bitterness that goes well with the tastes of pesto sauce and a hint of prosciutto. You could also try this combination with Belgian endive in place of the radicchio. For a vegetarian version, feel free to leave out the prosciutto.

Prebaked pizza crust	6-inch	12-inch
Pesto sauce	3 tablespoons	¾ cup
Small head radicchio	1	4
Thinly sliced prosciutto	1 ounce	¼ pound
Shredded fontina cheese	1½ ounces	6 ounces
Shredded mozzarella cheese	1 ounce	¼ pound
Fresh parsley, chopped fine	½ tablespoon	2 tablespoons

Preheat the oven to 450°F. Place the pizza crust on a baking sheet.

Spread the pesto sauce on top of the crust up to ½ inch from its edge.

Cut the radicchio crosswise into ¼-inch-thick slices. Arrange them on top of the sauce. Cut the prosciutto into thin slivers and scatter them over the radicchio. Spread evenly with the fontina and mozzarella.

Bake the pizza until the cheese is bubbly and just beginning to brown, about 10 minutes. Remove from the oven, transfer to a cutting board, garnish with parsley, and cut into slices.

Garlic Salami with Ricotta

MAKES 1 6-INCH PIZZA (*serves 1*) *or* 1 12-INCH PIZZA (*serves 4–6*)

For this pizza, seek out a really flavorful garlic salami from a good Italian delicatessen. I like the way the sweet, mild flavor of the ricotta plays off the power of the sausage.

Prebaked pizza crust	6-inch	12-inch
Pizza sauce	3 tablespoons	¾ cup
Freshly grated Parmesan cheese	1 tablespoon	¼ cup
Ricotta cheese	6 tablespoons	1½ cups
Garlicky Italian salami	2 ounces	½ pound
Fresh basil, shredded fine	½ tablespoon	2 tablespoons

Preheat the oven to 450°F. Place the pizza crust on a baking sheet.

Spread the pizza sauce on top of the crust up to ½ inch from its edge. Sprinkle evenly with the Parmesan. Spread the ricotta evenly on top.

Cut the salami into ½-inch cubes and dot them evenly over the pizza, pressing them into the ricotta.

Bake the pizza until the cheese is bubbly and just beginning to brown, about 10 minutes. Remove from the oven, transfer to a cutting board, garnish with basil, and cut into slices.

Italian BLT

MAKES 1 6-INCH PIZZA (*serves 1*) *or* 1 12-INCH PIZZA (*serves 4–6*)

With pancetta, Roma tomatoes, and a final flourish of lightly dressed lettuce, this pizza approximates the taste combination of a bacon, lettuce, and tomato sandwich—with a vibrant Italian twist. If you can't find pancetta in an Italian delicatessen, substitute good-quality unsmoked bacon. You may find the pizza easier to eat with a knife and fork.

Prebaked pizza crust	*6-inch*	*12-inch*
Pizza sauce	3 tablespoons	¾ cup
Freshly grated Parmesan cheese	1 tablespoon	¼ cup
Pancetta (Italian bacon)	1½ ounces	6 ounces
Shredded mozzarella cheese	2 ounces	½ pound
Firm, ripe Roma tomato, sliced thin	1	4
Balsamic vinegar	1 teaspoon	4 teaspoons
Dijon-style mustard	¼ teaspoon	1 teaspoon
Salt and pepper to taste		
Extra-virgin olive oil	1 tablespoon	¼ cup
Romaine lettuce leaf	1	4

Preheat the oven to 450°F. Place the pizza crust on a baking sheet.

Spread the pizza sauce on top of the crust up to ½ inch from its edge. Sprinkle evenly with the Parmesan.

Heat a nonstick skillet over medium-high heat. Cut the pancetta into ¼-inch strips and sauté until lightly browned, 3 to 4 minutes. Drain on paper towels.

Scatter the pancetta strips over the pizza. Spread the mozzarella evenly over the surface; then arrange the tomato slices on top of the cheese.

Bake the pizza until the cheese has melted, about 10 minutes.

While the pizza bakes, stir together the vinegar, mustard, and salt and pepper to taste in a small bowl. Stirring continuously, pour in the olive oil in a thin, steady stream. Cut the lettuce crosswise into thin shreds. Toss with the dressing.

Remove the pizza from the oven, transfer to a cutting board, spread the lettuce on top, and cut into slices.

Mexicana with Chorizo and Chilies

MAKES 1 6-INCH PIZZA (*serves 1*) *or* 1 12-INCH PIZZA (*serves 4–6*)

If you'd like a milder version, substitute Spanish chorizo for the Mexican product, and use canned mild green roasted chilies (most widely available under the Ortega brand) in place of the fresh jalapeño. You could also, if you wish, substitute heavy cream or crème fraîche for the pizza sauce. When handling any hot chili, take care to avoid touching your eyes, any cuts or abrasions, or any other sensitive areas, as the volatile oils can cause severe irritation; you might want to protect your hands with kitchen gloves. If not, be sure to wash your hands thoroughly with warm, soapy water afterward.

Prebaked pizza crust	*6-inch*	*12-inch*
Pizza sauce	*3 tablespoons*	*¾ cup*
Freshly grated Parmesan cheese	*1 tablespoon*	*¼ cup*
Jalapeño chili, stemmed, seeded, and chopped fine	*¼*	*1*
Mexican chorizo sausage	*¼ pound*	*1 pound*
Feta cheese, crumbled	*1½ ounces*	*6 ounces*
Shredded Monterey Jack cheese	*2 ounces*	*½ pound*
Cilantro, chopped fine	*1 teaspoon*	*4 teaspoons*

Preheat the oven to 450°F. Place the pizza crust on a baking sheet.

Spread the pizza sauce on top of the crust up to ½ inch from its edge. Sprinkle evenly with the Parmesan and then the chopped jalapeño.

With a small sharp knife, slit the casing of the chorizo and peel it off. Coarsely crumble the sausage into a nonstick frying pan and fry over medium heat, stirring with a wooden spoon, until lightly browned, 3 to 5 minutes. Pour off and discard the fat and drain the sausage briefly on paper towels.

Scatter the chorizo pieces and feta cheese over the pizza. Spread evenly with the Monterey Jack.

Bake the pizza until the cheese has melted and is just beginning to brown, about 10 minutes. Remove from the oven, transfer to a cutting board, garnish with cilantro, and cut into slices.

Hawaiian-Style with Ham, Pineapple, and Monterey Jack

MAKES 1 6-INCH PIZZA (*serves 1*) *or* 1 12-INCH PIZZA (*serves 4–6*)

I've never been a great fan of pineapple on pizza; but I'll admit to having several friends here in California who like it. This pizza is dedicated to them. If you're like me, however, you might want to consider leaving the pineapple out!

Prebaked pizza crust	*6-inch*	*12-inch*
Grainy mustard	*1 tablespoon*	*4 tablespoons*
Heavy cream	*½ tablespoon*	*2 tablespoons*
Honey	*½ teaspoon*	*2 teaspoons*
Well-drained canned crushed pineapple	*2 tablespoons*	*½ cup*
Smoked ham, cut into ¼-inch dice	*2 ounces*	*½ pound*
Red bell pepper, stemmed, seeded, and diced	*¼*	*1*
Shredded Monterey Jack cheese	*2 ounces*	*½ pound*
Fresh chives, chopped fine	*½ teaspoon*	*2 teaspoons*

Preheat the oven to 450°F. Place the pizza crust on a baking sheet.

In a small bowl, stir together the mustard, cream, and honey and spread on top of the pizza crust up to ½ inch from its edge. Spread the crushed pineapple on top; then scatter with the diced ham and bell pepper. Sprinkle evenly with the cheese.

Bake the pizza until the cheese is bubbly and just beginning to brown, about 10 minutes. Remove from the oven and garnish with the chives. Transfer to a cutting board and cut into slices.

Sloppy Joes

MAKES 1 6-INCH PIZZA (*serves 1*) *or* 1 12-INCH PIZZA (*serves 4–6*)

A popular children's midweek dinner, traditionally served on burger buns, becomes a perfect quick topping for prebaked pizza crusts. Make it completely with beef, if you prefer; or try ground-turkey sloppy joes.

Prebaked pizza crust	6-inch	12-inch
Vegetable oil	½ tablespoon	2 tablespoons
Onion, chopped fine	2 tablespoons	½ cup
Green bell pepper, chopped fine	2 tablespoons	½ cup
Garlic, chopped fine	¼ teaspoon	1 teaspoon
Lean ground pork	2 ounces	½ pound
Lean ground beef	2 ounces	½ pound
Canned crushed tomatoes	¼ cup	1 cup
Cornstarch	½ teaspoon	2 teaspoons
Tomato paste	1 teaspoon	4 teaspoons
Worcestershire sauce	½ teaspoon	2 teaspoons
Dark brown sugar	½ teaspoon	2 teaspoons
Hot pepper sauce	¼ teaspoon	1 teaspoon
Salt and pepper to taste		
Shredded American cheese	2 ounces	½ pound

Preheat the oven to 450°F. Place the pizza crust on a baking sheet.

Heat the oil in a skillet over medium heat. Add the onion, green pepper, and garlic and sauté until the onion and garlic are translucent, 2 to 3 minutes. Add the pork and beef and sauté until evenly browned, about 5 minutes, stirring with a wooden spoon to break up the meat into small particles.

Drain off some of the liquid from the tomatoes into a small bowl. Stir in the cornstarch until dissolved.

Stir into the meat mixture the remaining tomatoes, tomato paste, Worcestershire sauce, brown sugar, and hot pepper sauce. Stir in the dissolved cornstarch and continue to cook, stirring frequently, until the mixture reduces to a thick consistency. Season to taste with salt and pepper.

Spread the sloppy joe mixture evenly over the pizza crust up to ½ inch from its edge. Sprinkle the American cheese evenly on top.

Bake the pizza until the cheese is bubbly and just beginning to brown, about 10 minutes. Remove from the oven, transfer to a cutting board, and cut into slices.

Ground Beef and Onion

MAKES 1 6-INCH PIZZA (*serves 1*) *or* 1 12-INCH PIZZA (*serves 4–6*)

In this recipe, the ground beef mixture includes its own sauce. Try substituting some ground pork for part of the beef, if you wish.

Prebaked pizza crust	6-inch	12-inch
Olive oil	½ tablespoon	2 tablespoons
Onion, chopped fine	¼ cup	1 cup
Garlic clove, chopped fine	½	2
Lean ground beef	¼ pound	1 pound
Canned tomato sauce	3 tablespoons	¾ cup
Fresh parsley, chopped fine	½ teaspoon	2 teaspoons
Sugar	½ teaspoon	2 teaspoons
Salt and pepper to taste		
Shredded cheddar cheese	1 ounce	¼ pound
Shredded mozzarella cheese	1 ounce	¼ pound

Preheat the oven to 450°F. Place the pizza crust on a baking sheet.

Heat the olive oil in a skillet over medium heat. Add the onion and garlic and sauté until translucent, 2 to 3 minutes. Add the meat and sauté until evenly browned, about 5 minutes, stirring with a wooden spoon to break up the meat into small particles.

Stir in the tomato sauce, parsley, and sugar and cook, stirring frequently, until the mixture reduces to a thick sauce. Season to taste with salt and pepper.

Spread the beef-and-onion mixture evenly over the pizza crust up to ½ inch from its edge. Sprinkle the cheddar and mozzarella evenly on top.

Bake the pizza until the cheese is bubbly and just beginning to brown, about 10 minutes. Remove from the oven, transfer to a cutting board, and cut into slices.

Picadillo-Style Ground Beef

MAKES 1 6-INCH PIZZA (*serves 1*) *or* 1 12-INCH PIZZA (*serves 4–6*)

Readily available fresh chili peppers add lively spice to this quickly sautéed, Mexican-inspired pizza topping. If you like, substitute ground turkey for the beef; and make it healthier still by using reduced-fat cheese.

Prebaked pizza crust	6-inch	12-inch
Olive oil	½ tablespoon	2 tablespoons
Onion, chopped fine	2 tablespoons	½ cup
Small green chili, chopped fine	½	2
Garlic clove, chopped fine	½	2
Chili powder	⅛ teaspoon	½ teaspoon
Lean ground beef	¼ pound	1 pound
Firm, ripe Roma tomato, chopped	1	4
Dried oregano	¼ teaspoon	1 teaspoon
Sugar	¼ teaspoon	1 teaspoon
Salt and pepper to taste		
Shredded Monterey Jack cheese	2 ounces	½ pound

Preheat the oven to 450°F. Place the pizza crust on a baking sheet.

Heat the olive oil in a skillet over medium heat. Add the onion, green chili, and garlic and sauté until the onion and garlic are translucent, 2 to 3 minutes. Stir in the chili powder and sauté about 30 seconds more. Add the meat and sauté until evenly browned, about 5 minutes, stirring with a wooden spoon to break up the meat into small particles.

Stir in the tomato, oregano, and sugar and cook, stirring frequently, until the mixture reduces to a thick sauce. Season to taste with salt and pepper.

Spread the beef mixture evenly over the pizza crust up to ½ inch from its edge. Sprinkle the Monterey Jack evenly on top.

Bake the pizza until the cheese is bubbly and just beginning to brown, about 10 minutes. Remove from the oven, transfer to a cutting board, and cut into slices.

Moroccan Lamb

MAKES 1 6-INCH PIZZA (*serves 1*) *or* 1 12-INCH PIZZA (*serves 4–6*)

The spicing in this quickly sautéed topping of ground lamb may taste a trifle exotic; but the flavors perfectly complement the rich taste of the meat, and you'll find them surprisingly winning.

Prebaked pizza crust	6-inch	12-inch
Unsalted butter	½ tablespoon	2 tablespoons
Onion, chopped fine	¼ cup	1 cup
Garlic clove, chopped fine	½	2
Ground cinnamon	⅛ teaspoon	½ teaspoon
Ground ginger	⅛ teaspoon	½ teaspoon
Hot paprika	⅛ teaspoon	½ teaspoon
Lean ground lamb	¼ pound	1 pound
Firm, ripe Roma tomato, chopped fine	1	4
Seedless raisins	1 tablespoon	¼ cup
Sugar	½ teaspoon	2 teaspoons
Fresh parsley, chopped fine	½ tablespoon	2 tablespoons
Grated lemon zest	½ teaspoon	2 teaspoons
Salt and pepper to taste		
Shredded fontina cheese	2 ounces	½ pound
Pine nuts	1 tablespoon	¼ cup
Fresh mint, chopped fine	½ tablespoon	2 tablespoons

Preheat the oven to 450°F. Place the pizza crust on a baking sheet.

Heat the butter in a skillet over medium heat. Add the onion and garlic and sauté until translucent, 2 to 3 minutes. Add the cinnamon, ginger, and paprika and sauté about 30 seconds more. Add the lamb and sauté until evenly browned, about 5 minutes, stirring with a wooden spoon to break up the meat into small particles.

Stir in the tomato, raisins, and sugar and cook, stirring frequently, until the mixture is thick, about 10 minutes. Stir in the parsley and lemon zest and season to taste with salt and pepper.

Spread the lamb mixture evenly over the pizza crust up to ½ inch from its edge. Sprinkle the fontina cheese evenly on top and then scatter the pine nuts over the cheese.

Bake the pizza until the cheese is bubbly and just beginning to brown, about 10 minutes. Remove from the oven, transfer to a cutting board, garnish with mint, and cut into slices.

The Ultimate Barbecued Chicken with Roasted Peppers, Sweet Onion, and Smoked Cheeses

MAKES 1 6-INCH PIZZA (*serves 1*) *or* 1 12-INCH PIZZA (*serves 4–6*)

I find that smoked cheese gives this version of the now-familiar barbecued chicken pizza another rich dimension of flavor that elevates it far beyond the usual. Use your favorite bottled brand of sweet tomato-based barbecue sauce. If you want to make the pizza even easier, use smoked chicken (or one of the barbecued chickens commonly sold in large supermarkets) instead of cooking the poultry yourself. Feel free to use any smoked cheeses that you like.

Prebaked pizza crust	*6-inch*	*12-inch*
Boneless, skinless chicken breast	¼ pound	1 pound
Vegetable oil	1 tablespoon	4 tablespoons
Garlic clove, chopped fine	1 small	2 large
Salt and pepper to taste		
Sweet tomato-based barbecue sauce	¼ cup	1 cup
Small red onion, sliced thin	½	2
Roasted red bell pepper	½	2
Shredded smoked cheddar cheese	1 ounce	¼ pound
Shredded smoked gouda cheese	1 ounce	¼ pound
Fresh chives, chopped fine	½ teaspoon	2 teaspoons
Fresh parsley, chopped fine	½ teaspoon	2 teaspoons

Preheat the oven to 450°F. Place the pizza crust on a baking sheet.

Cut the chicken crosswise into ¼-inch-thick slices. In a frying pan large enough to hold the chicken pieces comfortably in a single layer, heat the oil and the garlic over high heat. As soon as the garlic sizzles, add the chicken, season to taste with salt and pepper, and sauté just until it loses its pink color, about 1 minute. Add about one fourth of the barbecue sauce and sauté about 1 minute more, until it thickly coats the chicken pieces.

Spread the remaining sauce on top of the pizza crust up to ½ inch from its edge. Arrange the red onion on top of the sauce and distribute the chicken pieces on top of the onion. Tear the roasted pepper into thin strips and scatter them over the pizza. Sprinkle evenly with the smoked cheeses.

Bake the pizza until the cheese is bubbly and just beginning to brown, about 10 minutes. Remove from the oven and garnish with the chives and parsley. Transfer to a cutting board and cut into slices.

Seared Chicken with Sautéed Leeks and Dolcelatte

MAKES 1 6-INCH PIZZA (*serves 1*) *or* 1 12-INCH PIZZA (*serves 4–6*)

You'll find this combination of flavors particularly rich and satisfying, with the chicken highlighted by the oniony sweetness of the buttery leeks and the sweet tang of dolcelatte, literally "sweet milk," a particularly mild form of Italy's gorgonzola cheese.

Prebaked pizza crust	*6-inch*	*12-inch*
Unsalted butter	*2 tablespoons*	*½ cup*
Small leak, white part only, washed and sliced thin	*1*	*4*
Salt and white pepper to taste		
Olive oil	*1 tablespoon*	*¼ cup*
Boneless, skinless chicken breast	*¼ pound*	*1 pound*
Dolcelatte cheese	*2 ounces*	*½ pound*
Shredded fontina cheese	*1 ounce*	*¼ pound*
Fresh chives, chopped fine	*½ teaspoon*	*2 teaspoons*
Fresh parsley, chopped fine	*½ teaspoon*	*2 teaspoons*

Preheat the oven to 450°F. Place the pizza crust on a baking sheet.

In a frying pan, melt the butter over moderate heat. Add the leek slices and sauté until tender, 5 to 7 minutes. Season to taste with salt and pepper. Spread the leek slices on top of the pizza crust up to ½ inch from its edge.

Wipe out the pan with paper towels and heat the oil in it over medium-to-high heat. Season the chicken breast with salt and white pepper and cook until seared deep golden brown, 2 to 3 minutes per side. Remove from the pan and cut crosswise into ¼-inch-thick slices (they'll still be slightly pink inside).

Distribute the chicken slices evenly over the pizza, nestling them down into the bed of leeks. Dot the dolcelatte evenly on top and sprinkle evenly with the fontina.

Bake the pizza until the cheese is bubbly and just beginning to brown, about 10 minutes. Remove from the oven and garnish with the chives and parsley. Transfer to a cutting board and cut into slices.

Chicken Fajitas

MAKES 1 6-INCH PIZZA (*serves 1*) *or* 1 12-INCH PIZZA (*serves 4–6*)

Think of a prebaked pizza crust as the equivalent of a very thick flour tortilla, and you can instantly understand why the Southwestern favorite known as fajitas works so well as a topping. Consider substituting good-quality steak for the chicken.

Prebaked pizza crust	6-inch	12-inch
Pizza sauce	2 tablespoons	½ cup
Boneless, skinless chicken breast	¼ pound	1 pound
Olive oil	1 tablespoon	¼ cup
Small red onion, sliced thin	½	1 large
Green bell pepper, sliced thin	¼	1
Jalapeño chili, sliced thin	¼	1
Salt and pepper to taste		
Lime juice	½ teaspoon	1 teaspoon
Feta cheese	1 ounce	¼ pound
Shredded Monterey Jack cheese	2 ounces	½ pound
Medium-sized ripe avocado, peeled, pitted, and cut into thin lengthwise slices	¼	1
Cilantro, chopped fine	½ tablespoon	2 tablespoons

Preheat the oven to 450°F. Place the pizza crust on a baking sheet. Spread the pizza sauce on top of the crust up to ½ inch from its edge.

Cut the chicken breast crosswise into ¼-inch-thick pieces.

In a heavy nonstick frying pan large enough to hold the ingredients without crowding, heat the oil over medium-to-high heat. Spread the onion, bell pepper, and chili evenly in the skillet and let sear for about 1 minute. Add the chicken, sprinkle with salt and pepper to taste, and sauté just until seared on all sides, 3 to 4 minutes. Sprinkle with the lime juice, stir briefly, and remove from the heat.

Distribute the chicken, the vegetables, and their juices evenly over the sauce. Crumble the feta on top, then spread evenly with the Monterey Jack.

Bake the pizza until the cheese has melted and begun to brown slightly, about 10 minutes. Remove from the oven, garnish with avocado and cilantro, transfer to a cutting board, and cut into slices.

Smoked Chicken with Pesto, Red Onions, and Provolone

MAKES 1 6-INCH PIZZA (*serves 1*) or 1 12-INCH PIZZA (*serves 4–6*)

Subtle savors permeate this easy pizza. Well-stocked delicatessens and supermarket deli sections carry smoked chicken. You could substitute smoked turkey, if necessary.

Prebaked pizza crust	*6-inch*	*12-inch*
Pesto sauce	*3 tablespoons*	*¾ cup*
Smoked chicken breast, cut into thin strips	*3 ounces*	*¾ pound*
Small red onion, sliced very thin	*¼*	*1*
Shredded provolone cheese	*3 ounces*	*¾ pound*
Fresh parsley, chopped fine	*½ tablespoon*	*2 tablespoons*

Preheat the oven to 450°F. Place the pizza crust on a baking sheet.

Spread the pesto sauce on top of the crust up to ½ inch from its edge. Scatter the smoked chicken strips on top, and strew with the onions. Sprinkle evenly with the provolone.

Bake the pizza until the cheese is bubbly and just beginning to brown, about 10 minutes. Remove from the oven, transfer to a cutting board, garnish with parsley, and cut into slices.

Ham and Aged Provolone
with Mustard Cream

MAKES 1 6-INCH PIZZA (*serves 1*) *or* 1 12-INCH PIZZA (*serves 4–6*)

Think of this as a ham-and-cheese sandwich transformed into a pizza. Use any good-quality fully cooked ham you like. You can invent endless variations, substituting a favorite cheese or adding any number of embellishments—thinly sliced pickles, well-drained sauerkraut, or roasted bell peppers, to name but three—beneath the ham.

Prebaked pizza crust	*6-inch*	*12-inch*
Creamy Dijon-style mustard	*1 tablespoon*	*4 tablespoons*
Heavy cream	*½ tablespoon*	*2 tablespoons*
Smoked ham, sliced thin	*2 ounces*	*½ pound*
Shredded provolone cheese	*2 ounces*	*½ pound*
Fresh chives, chopped fine	*½ teaspoon*	*2 teaspoons*

Preheat the oven to 450°F. Place the pizza crust on a baking sheet.

In a small bowl, stir together the mustard and cream and spread on top of the pizza crust up to ½ inch from its edge. Arrange the sliced ham on top and sprinkle evenly with the cheese.

Bake the pizza until the cheese is bubbly and just beginning to brown, about 10 minutes. Remove from the oven and garnish with the chives. Transfer to a cutting board and cut into slices.

Chinese Minced Chicken

MAKES 1 6-INCH PIZZA (*serves 1*) *or* 1 12-INCH PIZZA (*serves 4–6*)

Ordinarily a mixture such as this would be spooned into iceberg lettuce leaves to be eaten taco-style as an appetizer at a Chinese meal. It lends itself very well, however, to a prebaked pizza crust. You can try the same recipe with pork. You'll find all the special ingredients in an Asian market or the Asian foods section of a well-stocked supermarket.

Prebaked pizza crust	*6-inch*	*12-inch*
Hoisin sauce	*3 tablespoons*	*¾ cup*
Peanut oil or vegetable oil	*½ tablespoon*	*2 tablespoons*
Grated fresh ginger	*½ teaspoon*	*2 teaspoons*
Garlic clove, chopped fine	*½*	*2*
Ground chicken breast	*¼ pound*	*1 pound*
Chopped canned water chestnuts	*1 tablespoon*	*¼ cup*
Black bean sauce	*1 tablespoon*	*¼ cup*
Dry sherry	*½ tablespoon*	*2 tablespoons*
Chicken broth	*½ tablespoon*	*2 tablespoons*
Soy sauce	*1 teaspoon*	*4 teaspoons*
Cornstarch	*½ teaspoon*	*2 teaspoons*
Scallion, white part only, sliced thin	*1*	*4*
Shredded fontina cheese	*2 ounces*	*½ pound*
Pine nuts	*½ tablespoon*	*2 tablespoons*
Cilantro, chopped fine	*½ tablespoon*	*2 tablespoons*

Preheat the oven to 450°F. Place the pizza crust on a baking sheet. Spread the hoisin sauce on the pizza crust up to ½ inch from its edge.

Heat the oil with the ginger and garlic in a skillet over medium heat. When the ginger and garlic sizzle, add the chicken and sauté until evenly browned, about 5 minutes, stirring with a wooden spoon to break up the meat into small particles. Stir in the water chestnuts and black bean sauce and sauté about 1 minute more.

Meanwhile, stir together the sherry, chicken broth, soy sauce, and cornstarch until the cornstarch is fully dissolved. Pour the mixture into the pan and stir well until the liquid thickens and coats the chicken, about 30 seconds.

Spread the chicken mixture evenly over the pizza crust. Scatter the scallion slices on top, sprinkle evenly with the fontina, and top with pine nuts.

Bake the pizza until the cheese is bubbly and just beginning to brown, about 10 minutes. Remove from the oven, transfer to a cutting board, garnish with cilantro, and cut into slices.

Southwestern Turkey

MAKES 1 6-INCH PIZZA (*serves 1*) *or* 1 12-INCH PIZZA (*serves 4–6*)

Favorite Southwestern seasonings combine with fresh salsa—widely available in supermarket refrigerated cases—and a trio of cheeses to give ground turkey a real punch. If you'd like to elaborate on the presentation even further, you could add thin slices of ripe avocado, pitted black olives, and even pickled jalapeño chilies.

Prebaked pizza crust	6-inch	12-inch
Fresh salsa, drained of excess liquid	3 tablespoons	¾ cup
Olive oil	½ tablespoon	2 tablespoons
Garlic clove, chopped fine	½	2
Pure chili powder	¼ teaspoon	1 teaspoon
Ground cumin	¼ teaspoon	1 teaspoon
Ground turkey	¼ pound	1 pound
Canned sweet corn	2 tablespoons	¼ cup
Canned chopped mild green chilies	1 tablespoon	¼ cup
Feta cheese	1 ounce	¼ pound
Shredded mozzarella cheese	1 ounce	¼ pound
Shredded Monterey Jack cheese	1 ounce	¼ pound
Sour cream	½ tablespoon	2 tablespoons
Cilantro, chopped fine	½ tablespoon	2 tablespoons

Preheat the oven to 450°F. Place the pizza crust on a baking sheet. Spread the salsa on the pizza crust up to ½ inch from its edge.

Heat the oil with the garlic in a skillet over medium heat. When the garlic sizzles, add the chili powder and cumin and sauté about 30 seconds more; then add the turkey and sauté until evenly browned, about 5 minutes, stirring with a wooden spoon to break up the turkey into small particles. Stir in the corn and chopped chilies and sauté about 1 minute more.

Spread the turkey mixture evenly over the pizza crust. Crumble the feta on top, then sprinkle evenly with the mozzarella and Monterey Jack.

Bake the pizza until the cheese is bubbly and just beginning to brown, about 10 minutes. Remove from the oven, transfer to a cutting board, garnish with sour cream and cilantro, and cut into slices.

Day-After-Thanksgiving Pizza

MAKES 1 6-INCH PIZZA (*serves 1*) *or* 1 12-INCH PIZZA (*serves 4–6*)

Try this simple pizza after Thanksgiving or any major holiday that calls for roast turkey and you'll wonder why no one ever thought of it before. Use your choice of leftover white or dark meat, slicing it as thin as possible. And, thanks to the widespread availability of roast turkey breast in supermarket delis, you don't even have to wait for Thanksgiving to make this delicious quick pizza. It also tastes good with sliced cooked ham, from your own kitchen or from the deli. If you'd like an edge of sharpness, spread a little creamy Dijon-style mustard on the crust before adding the cranberry sauce.

Prebaked pizza crust	6-inch	12-inch
Jellied or whole cranberry sauce	3 tablespoons	¾ cup
Cooked turkey, sliced thin	3 ounces	¾ pound
Shredded provolone cheese	1½ ounces	6 ounces
Shredded mozzarella cheese	1½ ounces	6 ounces
Fresh chives, chopped fine	1 teaspoon	4 teaspoons
Fresh parsley, chopped fine	1 teaspoon	4 teaspoons

Preheat the oven to 450°F. Place the pizza crust on a baking sheet.

Spread the cranberry sauce on top of the crust up to ½ inch from its edge. Arrange the sliced turkey on top. Spread the provolone and mozzarella evenly over the top.

Bake the pizza until the cheese is bubbly and just beginning to brown, about 10 minutes. Remove from the oven, transfer to a cutting board, garnish with chives and parsley, and cut into slices.

Monte Cristo with Turkey, Ham, Provolone, and Dijon Cream

MAKES 1 6-INCH PIZZA *(serves 1)* or 1 12-INCH PIZZA *(serves 4–6)*

The elements of the popular Monte Cristo sandwich translate well to prebaked pizza crusts. Use the best-quality deli-sliced meats you can find.

Prebaked pizza crust	*6-inch*	*12-inch*
Creamy Dijon-style mustard	*1½ tablespoons*	*6 tablespoons*
Heavy cream	*1½ tablespoons*	*6 tablespoons*
Grated Parmesan cheese	*1 tablespoon*	*¼ cup*
Cooked turkey breast, sliced thin	*1½ ounces*	*6 ounces*
Shredded provolone cheese	*3 ounces*	*¾ pound*
Cooked smoked ham, sliced thin	*1½ ounces*	*6 ounces*
Fresh chives, chopped fine	*½ tablespoon*	*2 tablespoons*

Preheat the oven to 450°F. Place the pizza crust on a baking sheet.

In a bowl, stir together the mustard and cream. Spread the mustard cream on top of the crust up to ½ inch from its edge and sprinkle evenly with the Parmesan.

Arrange the sliced turkey on top and distribute about one third of the provolone over the turkey. Top with the ham and sprinkle evenly with the remaining cheese.

Bake the pizza until the cheese is melted and just beginning to brown, about 10 minutes. Remove from the oven, transfer to a cutting board, garnish with chives, and cut into slices.

CHAPTER FOUR

Seafood Toppings

Spicy Shrimp Scampi

Greek-Style Shrimp with Olive Oil, Oregano, Feta, and Tomatoes

Shrimp with Roasted Peppers, Pine Nuts, and Pesto

Japanese-Style Miso Shrimp

Crab with Zesty Tomato Sauce and Fontina

Tropical Crab with Mango and Chilies

Seared Scallops with Goat Cheese, Bacon, and Spinach

Garlic Clams with Fontina and Mozzarella

Smoked Mussels with Roasted Pepper

Taramasalata

For Anchovy Lovers

Anchovy Puttanesca

Tuna Melt Italiano

Tonno e Fagioli

Niçoise with Tuna, Black Olives, Capers, and Anchovies

Smoked Salmon with Crème Fraîche, Caviar, and Chives

Bagel-Style Lox with Cream Cheese, Red Onion, Tomato, and Lemon Zest

Four Seas

Spicy Shrimp Scampi

MAKES 1 6-INCH PIZZA *(serves 1)* or 1 12-INCH PIZZA *(serves 4–6)*

Crushed garlic and red pepper flakes add wonderful aroma to the shrimp topping for this pizza. To elaborate on it, add roasted pepper strips or thin rings of onion over the shrimp before you add the cheese.

Prebaked pizza crust	6-inch	12-inch
Pizza sauce	3 tablespoons	¾ cup
Extra-virgin olive oil	1 tablespoon	¼ cup
Large garlic clove, chopped fine	1	4
Crushed red pepper flakes	¼ teaspoon	1 teaspoon
Medium-sized shrimp, peeled and deveined	4	16
Salt and pepper to taste		
Fresh goat cheese, at room temperature	1 ounce	¼ pound
Shredded fontina cheese	2 ounces	½ pound

Preheat the oven to 450°F. Place the pizza crust on a baking sheet.

Spread the pizza sauce on top of the crust up to ½ inch from its edge.

In a frying pan, heat the olive oil with the garlic and red pepper flakes over medium-high heat. As soon as the garlic sizzles, add the shrimp and sauté just until they turn pink, about 1 minute. Add salt and pepper to taste.

Arrange the shrimp on top of the pizza. With a spoon, drizzle the garlic, pepper flakes, and oil over the pizza. Dot small clusters of goat cheese over the surface, then sprinkle evenly with the fontina.

Bake the pizza until the cheese has melted and is just beginning to brown, about 10 minutes. Remove from the oven, transfer to a cutting board, and cut into slices.

Greek-Style Shrimp with Olive Oil, Oregano, Feta, and Tomatoes

MAKES 1 6-INCH PIZZA (*serves 1*) *or* 1 12-INCH PIZZA (*serves 4–6*)

Mozzarella excluded, the ingredients used in this topping are identical to those used in one of the most popular shrimp dishes favored in Greek tavernas. The fragrant olive oil in which the shrimp are quickly sautéed becomes the sauce for the pizza.

Prebaked pizza crust	6-inch	12-inch
Medium-to-large fresh shrimp	4	16
Extra-virgin olive oil	1 tablespoon	¼ cup
Garlic clove, chopped fine	1 small	2 large
Fresh oregano, chopped fine	½ teaspoon	2 teaspoons
Salt and white pepper to taste		
Lemon juice	1 teaspoon	4 teaspoons
Firm, ripe Roma tomato, chopped coarse	½	2
Feta cheese	2 ounces	½ pound
Shredded mozzarella cheese	1 ounce	¼ pound

Preheat the oven to 450°F. Place the pizza crust on a baking sheet.

Peel and devein the shrimp and cut them in half lengthwise.

In a frying pan, heat the oil with the garlic over medium heat. As soon as the garlic sizzles, add the shrimp and sauté just until they turn pink, about 1 minute. Stir in the oregano and season to taste with salt and white pepper. Remove from the heat and sprinkle in the lemon juice.

Arrange the shrimp on top of the pizza crust, spooning the juices from the pan evenly over the crust up to ½ inch from its edge. Scatter the tomato on top. Crumble the feta over the pizza and sprinkle evenly with the mozzarella.

Bake the pizza until the cheese is melted, about 10 minutes. Remove from the oven, transfer to a cutting board, and cut into slices.

Shrimp with Roasted Peppers, Pine Nuts, and Pesto

MAKES 1 6-INCH PIZZA (serves 1) or 1 12-INCH PIZZA (serves 4–6)

Vibrantly Mediterranean in its combination of flavors, this pizza is especially quick and easy to make if you use bottled roasted peppers from an Italian delicatessen or well-stocked supermarket. If you wish, substitute pizza sauce for the pesto.

Prebaked pizza crust	6-inch	12-inch
Pesto sauce	3 tablespoons	¾ cup
Extra-virgin olive oil	1 tablespoon	¼ cup
Medium-to-large fresh shrimp, peeled and deveined	4	16
Salt and white pepper to taste		
Lemon juice	1 teaspoon	4 teaspoons
Roasted red bell pepper	½	2
Shredded fontina cheese	2 ounces	½ pound
Shredded mozzarella cheese	1 ounce	¼ pound
Pine nuts	1 tablespoon	¼ cup
Fresh basil, shredded fine	½ tablespoon	2 tablespoons

Preheat the oven to 450°F. Place the pizza crust on a baking sheet. Spread the pesto sauce on top of the crust up to ½ inch from its edge.

In a frying pan, heat the oil. Season the shrimp to taste with salt and white pepper and toss with the lemon juice. Add to the pan and sauté just until they turn pink, about 1 minute.

Arrange the shrimp on top of the pizza crust. Tear the roasted pepper into thin strips and scatter them on top. Sprinkle the fontina and mozzarella cheeses evenly over the pizza. Scatter the pine nuts on top.

Bake the pizza until the cheese is melted and just beginning to brown, about 10 minutes. Remove from the oven, transfer to a cutting board, garnish with basil, and cut into slices.

Japanese-Style Miso Shrimp

MAKES 1 6-INCH PIZZA (*serves 1*) *or* 1 12-INCH PIZZA (*serves 4–6*)

The rich-tasting, salty-sweet Japanese fermented soybean paste known as miso makes a surprisingly good pizza sauce here. You'll find it in the refrigerated case of well-stocked supermarkets or in Asian shops. Use either the yellow (actually pale brown in color) or red (reddish brown) miso.

Prebaked pizza crust	6-inch	12-inch
Miso	3 tablespoons	¾ cup
Peanut oil or other vegetable oil	1 tablespoon	¼ cup
Medium-to-large fresh shrimp, peeled and deveined	4	16
Soy sauce	1 teaspoon	4 teaspoons
Scallion, white part only, sliced thin	½	2
Shredded fontina cheese	2 ounces	½ pound
Shredded mozzarella cheese	1 ounce	¼ pound
Mustard sprouts	1 tablespoon	¼ cup

Preheat the oven to 450°F. Place the pizza crust on a baking sheet. Spread the miso on top of the crust up to ½ inch from its edge.

In a frying pan, heat the oil. Toss the shrimp with the soy sauce; then add them to the pan and sauté just until they turn pink, about 1 minute.

Arrange the shrimp on the pizza crust. Scatter the scallion slices on top. Sprinkle the fontina and mozzarella evenly over the pizza.

Bake the pizza until the cheese is melted and just beginning to brown, about 10 minutes. Remove from the oven, transfer to a cutting board, garnish with sprouts, and cut into slices.

Crab with Zesty Tomato Sauce and Fontina

MAKES 1 6-INCH PIZZA (*serves 1*) *or* 1 12-INCH PIZZA (*serves 4–6*)

Most well-stocked fishmongers and supermarket seafood departments will sell you ready-cooked shelled crabmeat, which makes this luxurious-tasting pizza exceptionally easy to prepare. Try it instead, if you like, with tiny cooked bay shrimp.

Prebaked pizza crust	6-inch	12-inch
Pizza sauce	3 tablespoons	¾ cup
Grated lemon zest	1 teaspoon	4 teaspoons
Flaked crabmeat	2 ounces	½ pound
Shredded fontina cheese	2 ounces	½ pound
Shredded mozzarella cheese	1 ounce	¼ pound
Fresh basil, shredded fine	½ tablespoon	2 tablespoons

Preheat the oven to 450°F. Place the pizza crust on a baking sheet.

Spread the pizza sauce on top of the crust up to ½ inch from its edge. Sprinkle the sauce evenly with the lemon zest.

Pick over the crabmeat to remove any pieces of shell or gristle. Then spread the crabmeat evenly over the pizza. Sprinkle evenly with the fontina and mozzarella.

Bake the pizza until the cheese has melted and begun to brown slightly, about 10 minutes. Remove from the oven, transfer to a cutting board, garnish with basil, and cut into slices.

Tropical Crab with Mango and Chilies

MAKES 1 6-INCH PIZZA (*serves 1*) *or* 1 12-INCH PIZZA (*serves 4–6*)

A touch of exotic fruit gives this quick pizza an elusive sweetness. You could substitute papaya—or even fresh peach—for the mango.

Prebaked pizza crust	6-inch	12-inch
Fresh goat cheese, softened	1½ ounces	6 ounces
Flaked crabmeat	2 ounces	½ pound
Canned chopped mild green chilies	1 tablespoon	¼ cup
¼-inch-by-3-inch slices ripe mango	2	8
Shredded fontina cheese	1½ ounces	6 ounces
Cilantro, chopped fine	½ tablespoon	2 tablespoons

Preheat the oven to 450°F. Place the pizza crust on a baking sheet.

Spread the goat cheese on top of the crust up to ½ inch from its edge.

Pick over the crabmeat to remove any pieces of shell or gristle. Then spread the crabmeat evenly over the pizza. Sprinkle evenly with the chilies. Place the mango on top and spread evenly with the fontina.

Bake the pizza until the cheese has melted and begun to brown slightly, about 10 minutes. Remove from the oven, transfer to a cutting board, garnish with cilantro, and cut into slices.

Seared Scallops with Goat Cheese, Bacon, and Spinach

MAKES 1 6-INCH PIZZA (*serves 1*) *or* 1 12-INCH PIZZA (*serves 4–6*)

The inspiration for this quick pizza topping comes from salads I've enjoyed at my friend Michael McCarty's restaurant, Michael's, in Santa Monica, California. You can substitute pesto sauce for the pizza sauce, or shrimp for the scallops. And, if you prefer, the bacon may be left out—though it adds a hint of smoky taste that goes very well with the other ingredients.

Prebaked pizza crust	6-inch	12-inch
Pizza sauce	3 tablespoons	¾ cup
Large sea scallops, trimmed	4	16
Extra-virgin olive oil	½ tablespoon	2 tablespoons
Salt and white pepper to taste		
Smoked bacon, sliced thin	1 ounce	¼ pound
Packed baby spinach leaves, trimmed	¼ cup	1 cup
Fresh goat cheese, at room temperature	2 ounces	½ pound
Shredded mozzarella cheese	1 ounce	¼ pound

Preheat the oven to 450°F. Place the pizza crust on a baking sheet.

Spread the pizza sauce on top of the crust up to ½ inch from its edge.

Cut the scallops horizontally in halves to make 2 thin disks each. Toss with the olive oil and season to taste with salt and white pepper.

Heat a heavy nonstick frying pan over medium-high heat. Cut the bacon crosswise into ¼-inch pieces and sauté them until golden, 3 to 4 minutes. Drain on paper towels and pour the fat from the pan.

Over medium-high heat, add the scallops to the pan—in batches if necessary to prevent crowding—and sauté until seared light golden, about 30 seconds per side.

Scatter the spinach leaves over the surface of the pizza and arrange the scallops on top. Dot evenly with the goat cheese, scatter the bacon over the surface, and sprinkle evenly with the mozzarella.

Bake the pizza until the cheeses have melted and are just beginning to brown, about 10 minutes. Remove from the oven, transfer to a cutting board, and cut into slices.

Garlic Clams with Fontina and Mozzarella

MAKES 1 6-INCH PIZZA (*serves 1*) or 1 12-INCH PIZZA (*serves 4–6*)

Sweet-tasting fontina cheese moderates the sharp, briny flavor of rapidly sautéed clams in this true seafood-lover's pizza. If you'd like a spicier version, add a pinch or two of crushed red chili flakes along with the garlic.

Prebaked pizza crust	*6-inch*	*12-inch*
Unsalted butter	*1 tablespoon*	*4 tablespoons*
Extra-virgin olive oil	*1 tablespoon*	*¼ cup*
Large garlic clove, chopped fine	*1*	*4*
Canned whole clams, drained	*¼ cup*	*1 cup*
Fresh parsley, chopped fine	*1 teaspoon*	*1½ tablespoons*
Shredded fontina cheese	*2 ounces*	*½ pound*
Shredded mozzarella cheese	*1 ounce*	*¼ pound*

Preheat the oven to 450°F. Place the pizza crust on a baking sheet.

In a skillet, melt the butter in the oil over medium-high heat. Add the garlic; as soon as it gives off its aroma, stir in the clams. Sauté just until they turn opaque, about 1 minute. Stir in the parsley.

Spread the clam mixture evenly over the surface of the pizza crust up to ½ inch from its edge. Sprinkle the fontina and mozzarella cheeses evenly on top.

Bake the pizza until the cheeses are bubbly and just beginning to brown, about 10 minutes. Remove from the oven, transfer to a cutting board, and cut into slices.

Smoked Mussels with Roasted Pepper

MAKES 1 6-INCH PIZZA (*serves 1*) *or* 1 12-INCH PIZZA (*serves 4–6*)

Cans of plump, sweet little smoked mussels are available in well-stocked supermarkets and specialty food stores. Roasted red bell peppers, whether bought in the market or prepared at home, complement the seafood nicely. You can substitute smoked oysters for the mussels, or use tomato pizza sauce in place of the pesto.

Prebaked pizza crust	6-inch	12-inch
Pesto sauce	3 tablespoons	¾ cup
Canned smoked mussels	6	24
Roasted red bell pepper	¼	1
Shredded mozzarella cheese	2 ounces	½ pound
Shredded fontina cheese	1 ounce	¼ pound
Fresh basil, shredded fine	½ tablespoon	2 tablespoons

Preheat the oven to 450°F. Place the pizza crust on a baking sheet.

Spread the pesto sauce on top of the crust up to ½ inch from its edge. Arrange the mussels on top. Tear the pepper into thin strips and scatter over the mussels, then sprinkle evenly with the mozzarella and fontina.

Bake the pizza until the cheeses have melted and are just beginning to brown, about 10 minutes. Remove from the oven, transfer to a cutting board, garnish with basil, and cut into slices.

Taramasalata

MAKES 1 6-INCH PIZZA (*serves 1*) *or* 1 12-INCH PIZZA (*serves 4–6*)

A traditional Greek dip made from *tarama*, bright pinkish-orange salted cod's roe, the luscious dip known as taramasalata works brilliantly atop a prebaked pizza crust, which assumes the role usually taken by hot grilled pita bread. Even if you're preparing just one 6-inch pizza, I advise you to make the dip using the larger quantities below, so you'll have extra to serve the next day. You'll find tarama at Middle Eastern grocery stores; you can substitute the more widely available salmon roe, which has a similar color and a delicious flavor reminiscent of smoked salmon.

Prebaked pizza crust	6-inch	12-inch
Shredded fontina cheese	1 ounce	½ pound
Shredded mozzarella cheese	1 ounce	½ pound
Packed fresh sourdough bread crumbs	¼ cup	1 cup
Milk	3 tablespoons	¾ cup
Sweet onion, chopped fine	2 tablespoons	½ cup
Small garlic clove, chopped fine	1	4
Tarama or salmon roe	3 tablespoons	¾ cup
Lemon juice	½ tablespoon	2 tablespoons
Extra-virgin olive oil	¼ cup	1 cup
Salt and white pepper to taste		
Small scallion, sliced thin	½	2

Preheat the oven to 450°F. Place the pizza crust on a baking sheet. Spread the fontina and mozzarella evenly over the crust up to ½ inch from its edge.

Bake the pizza until the cheese has melted and begun to brown slightly, about 10 minutes.

While the pizza bakes, prepare the taramasalata. In a bowl, combine the bread crumbs and milk until the crumbs are uniformly moistened. With your hand, squeeze out excess liquid and put the crumbs in a food processor fitted with the metal blade. Add the onion and garlic and pulse the machine until the ingredients are finely pureed, scraping down the bowl once or twice. Add the tarama or salmon roe and process until smooth; then pulse in the lemon juice. With the machine running, pour in the olive oil in a thin stream, stopping when the mixture achieves the consistency of thick mayonnaise. Pulse in salt and white pepper to taste.

Remove the pizza from the oven and spread it with the taramasalata. Scatter the scallion slices on top and drizzle with the remaining olive oil. Cut into slices.

For Anchovy Lovers

MAKES 1 6-INCH PIZZA (*serves 1*) *or* 1 12-INCH PIZZA (*serves 4–6*)

I've included a generous amount of anchovies here, but if you're a real anchovy lover, you might well want to add more. Pesto sauce also goes very well with the recipe.

Prebaked pizza crust	*6-inch*	*12-inch*
Pizza sauce	*3 tablespoons*	*¾ cup*
Canned anchovy fillets	*4*	*16*
Shredded fontina cheese	*2 ounces*	*½ pound*
Shredded mozzarella cheese	*1 ounce*	*¼ pound*
Fresh basil, shredded fine	*½ teaspoon*	*2 teaspoons*
Fresh parsley, chopped fine	*½ teaspoon*	*2 teaspoons*

Preheat the oven to 450°F. Place the pizza crust on a baking sheet.

Spread the pizza sauce on top of the crust up to ½ inch from its edge. Arrange the anchovies on top and sprinkle evenly with the fontina and mozzarella.

Bake the pizza until the cheese is melted and just beginning to brown, about 10 minutes. Remove from the oven, garnish with basil and parsley, transfer to a cutting board, and cut into slices.

Anchovy Puttanesca

MAKES 1 6-INCH PIZZA (*serves 1*) *or* 1 12-INCH PIZZA (*serves 4–6*)

This pizza borrows its name from the Italian word for a woman of easy virtue, and its toppings from the similarly named pasta recipe.

Prebaked pizza crust	6-inch	12-inch
Pizza sauce	3 tablespoons	¾ cup
Garlic clove, chopped fine	1 small	2 large
Crushed red pepper flakes	¼ teaspoon	1 teaspoon
Fresh basil, shredded fine	½ teaspoon	2 teaspoons
Fresh parsley, chopped fine	½ teaspoon	2 teaspoons
Canned anchovy fillets, chopped coarse	3	12
Niçoise olives, pitted and halved	4	16
Small capers, drained	½ teaspoon	2 teaspoons
Fresh, creamy goat cheese	1 ounce	¼ pound
Shredded fontina cheese	2 ounces	½ pound

Preheat the oven to 450°F. Place the pizza crust on a baking sheet.

Spread the pizza sauce on top of the crust up to ½ inch from its edge. Sprinkle the garlic and red pepper flakes evenly over the sauce, then scatter the basil and parsley. Distribute the anchovies, olives, and capers evenly over the surface. Dot with the goat cheese, then sprinkle evenly with the fontina.

Bake the pizza until the cheese is melted and just beginning to brown, about 10 minutes. Remove from the oven, transfer to a cutting board, and cut into slices.

Tuna Melt Italiano

MAKES 1 6-INCH PIZZA (*serves 1*) *or* 1 12-INCH PIZZA (*serves 4–6*)

If you've ever tasted a tuna melt or a hot tuna grinder (or sub or hero), you already know the pleasures in store for you with this quickly prepared pizza. If not, you have a new treat ahead of you. Once you've made this a few times, you might want to try varying it by spreading a thin layer of pesto sauce on the crust before adding the other toppings. Once the pizza is out of the oven, you could also top it with a salad of finely shredded Romaine lettuce tossed with a balsamic vinaigrette or your favorite Italian dressing.

Prebaked pizza crust	6-inch	12-inch
Canned tuna, drained	3½ ounces	14 ounces
Mayonnaise	2 tablespoons	½ cup
Lemon juice	1 teaspoon	4 teaspoons
Dijon-style mustard	½ teaspoon	2 teaspoons
Small capers, drained	1 tablespoon	¼ cup
Fresh parsley, chopped fine	1 tablespoon	¼ cup
Fresh chives, chopped fine	1 tablespoon	¼ cup
Salt and white pepper to taste		
Freshly grated Parmesan cheese	1 ounce	¼ pound
Shredded mozzarella cheese	2 ounces	½ pound
Fresh basil, shredded fine	½ tablespoon	2 tablespoons

Preheat the oven to 450°F. Place the pizza crust on a baking sheet.

In a bowl, mash together the tuna, mayonnaise, lemon juice, and mustard until smooth. Stir in the capers, parsley, and chives and season to taste with salt and white pepper.

Sprinkle the Parmesan evenly over the pizza crust up to ½ inch from its edge. Spread the tuna salad evenly on top of the Parmesan. Sprinkle evenly with the mozzarella.

Bake the pizza until the cheese is melted and just beginning to brown, about 10 minutes. Remove from the oven, transfer to a cutting board, garnish with basil, and cut into slices.

Tonno e Fagioli

MAKES 1 6-INCH PIZZA (*serves 1*) *or* 1 12-INCH PIZZA (*serves 4–6*)

Canned tuna and white beans traditionally combine to make one of Italy's greatest antipasti. I use the combination here, along with pesto sauce and cheese, as a wonderfully quick topping for a prebaked pizza crust. You'll get the best, most authentic flavor by using imported Italian tuna canned in olive oil; but even your favorite brand of water-packed tuna will work fine. And don't worry if your canned tuna isn't the exact size as the quantities called for; just use approximately the same amount.

Prebaked pizza crust	*6-inch*	*12-inch*
Pesto sauce	3 tablespoons	¾ cup
Canned tuna, drained	3½ ounces	14 ounces
Canned cannellini or other white beans, drained	¼ cup	1 cup
Red onion, chopped fine	1 tablespoon	¼ cup
Lemon juice	½ teaspoon	2 teaspoons
Shredded fontina cheese	2 ounces	½ pound
Shredded mozzarella cheese	1 ounce	¼ pound
Fresh parsley, chopped fine	½ tablespoon	2 tablespoons

Preheat the oven to 450°F. Place the pizza crust on a baking sheet.

Spread the pesto sauce on top of the crust up to ½ inch from its edge. Break up the tuna into chunks and distribute them over the sauce; then scatter the beans on top. Sprinkle with the red onion and then the lemon juice. Sprinkle evenly with the fontina and mozzarella.

Bake the pizza until the cheese is melted and just beginning to brown, about 10 minutes. Remove from the oven, transfer to a cutting board, garnish with parsley, and cut into slices.

Niçoise with Tuna, Black Olives, Capers, and Anchovies

MAKES 1 6-INCH PIZZA (*serves 1*) *or* 1 12-INCH PIZZA (*serves 4–6*)

I think of this recipe as a quick pizza version of the classic *salade Niçoise*. If you can find it, use imported Italian tuna packed in olive oil. If you want to cut down on the calories, feel free to use water-packed tuna.

Prebaked pizza crust	6-inch	12-inch
Pizza sauce	3 tablespoons	¾ cup
Canned tuna, drained and broken into chunks	¼ cup	1 cup
Niçoise olives, pitted and halved	6	24
Small capers, drained	½ tablespoon	2 tablespoons
Canned anchovy fillets, chopped coarse	2	8
Shredded mozzarella cheese	2 ounces	½ pound
Fresh basil, shredded fine	½ tablespoon	2 tablespoons

Preheat the oven to 450°F. Place the pizza crust on a baking sheet.

Spread the pizza sauce on top of the crust up to ½ inch from its edge. Distribute the tuna, olives, capers, and anchovies evenly over the surface. Sprinkle evenly with the mozzarella.

Bake the pizza until the cheese is melted and just beginning to brown, about 10 minutes. Remove from the oven, garnish with basil, transfer to a cutting board, and cut into slices.

Smoked Salmon with Crème Fraîche, Caviar, and Chives

MAKES 1 6-INCH PIZZA (*serves 1*) *or* 1 12-INCH PIZZA (*serves 4–6*)

Legendary restaurateur Wolfgang Puck deserves credit for popularizing smoked salmon pizzas. In place of the crème fraîche, you can use equal parts heavy cream and sour cream. Use whatever kind of caviar is available and affordable to you, from relatively inexpensive golden caviar or salmon roe to expensive imported beluga, sevruga, or osetra. Serve with champagne or iced vodka.

Prebaked pizza crust	6-inch	12-inch
Crème fraîche	3 tablespoons	¾ cup
Smoked salmon, sliced thin	2 ounces	½ pound
Caviar	1 tablespoon	¼ cup
Fresh chives, chopped fine	½ tablespoon	2 tablespoons
Generous wedge lemon	1	4
Freshly ground black pepper to taste		

Preheat the oven to 450°F. Place the pizza crust on a baking sheet.

Spread the crème fraîche on top of the crust up to ½ inch from its edge. Bake the pizza until the crust is heated through and the crème fraîche is bubbly, about 10 minutes.

Remove the pizza from the oven. Immediately drape the smoked salmon on top and cut into slices. Then garnish each slice with small dollops of caviar and a scattering of chives. Serve with fresh lemon and black pepper added to taste.

Bagel-Style Lox with Cream Cheese, Red Onion, Tomato, and Lemon Zest

MAKES 1 6-INCH PIZZA (*serves 1*) *or* 1 12-INCH PIZZA (*serves 4–6*)

My favorite way of enjoying a bagel translates perfectly to prebaked pizza crusts. Vary the recipe any way you like—leaving off the onion or tomato, for example, or substituting chives, capers, or any other flourishes you prefer. You could, for example, top the lox with finely shredded lettuce leaves, or place some pitted and halved marinated black olives beneath the fish. I think this recipe works best with true deli-style lox because it is moister and more oily than smoked salmon, but you can certainly use fine smoked salmon if you wish.

Prebaked pizza crust	*6-inch*	*12-inch*
Cream cheese, softened	*3 tablespoons*	*¾ cup*
Small red onion, sliced thin	*¼*	*1*
Firm, ripe Roma tomato, sliced thin	*1*	*4*
Lox, sliced thin	*2 ounces*	*½ pound*
Grated lemon zest	*½ tablespoon*	*2 tablespoons*
Freshly ground black pepper to taste		

Preheat the oven to 450°F. Place the pizza crust on a baking sheet and bake until heated through and crisped, about 10 minutes.

Remove the crust from the oven and spread the cream cheese on top up to ½ inch from its edge. Arrange the red onion and tomato evenly on top of the cream cheese; then drape the lox over the vegetables. Sprinkle with lemon zest and black pepper to taste and cut into slices.

Four Seas

MAKES 1 6-INCH PIZZA (*serves 1*) *or* 1 12-INCH PIZZA (*serves 4–6*)

Forgive the pun. I think of this pizza as a seafood version of the classic Four Seasons pizza. (See Index.) And though one usually speaks of the *seven* seas, there are usually *four* ready-cooked (or cured) types of seafood commonly available to top a quick pizza. This recipe also works very well with pesto sauce.

Prebaked pizza crust	*6-inch*	*12-inch*
Pizza sauce	*3 tablespoons*	*¾ cup*
Freshly grated Parmesan cheese	*1 ounce*	*¼ pound*
Anchovies	*2*	*8*
Flaked crabmeat	*½ ounce*	*2 ounces*
Cooked bay shrimp	*½ ounce*	*2 ounces*
Canned tuna fish	*½ ounce*	*2 ounces*
Fresh parsley, chopped fine	*½ tablespoon*	*2 tablespoons*
Small capers, drained	*1 teaspoon*	*4 teaspoons*
Shredded fontina cheese	*1 ounce*	*¼ pound*
Shredded mozzarella cheese	*1 ounce*	*¼ pound*

Preheat the oven to 450°F. Place the pizza crust on a baking sheet.

Spread the pizza sauce on top of the crust up to ½ inch from its edge. Sprinkle the sauce evenly with the Parmesan.

On one quarter of the pizza, arrange each of the four types of seafood: the anchovies, left whole or broken up into pieces; the crabmeat, carefully picked over to remove any pieces of shell or gristle; the bay shrimp; and the tuna, broken into small chunks. Sprinkle evenly with the parsley; then scatter the capers on top. Spread evenly with the fontina and mozzarella.

Bake the pizza until the cheese has melted and begun to brown slightly, about 10 minutes. Remove from the oven, transfer to a cutting board, and cut into slices.

CHAPTER FIVE

Vegetable Toppings

Bruschetta-Style Pomodoro with Melted Parmesan

Cherry Tomatoes and Pesto

Sun-Dried Tomatoes with Ricotta

Rapid Spicy Tomato Sauté with Mozzarella

Roasted Peppers with Pesto and Ricotta

Crisp Bell Pepper Medley with Fontina and Smoked Mozzarella

Roasted Garlic

Garlic-Mushroom Sauté with Fontina

Asparagus Parmigiana

Charred Eggplant with Mozzarella and Basil

Texas-Style Grilled Corn

Four Seasons

Roasted Vegetables with Extra-Virgin Olive Oil

Spinach Salad with Garlic-Herb Cream Cheese

Arugula and Goat Cheese

Marinated Artichokes with Sun-Dried Tomatoes and Fontina

Marinated Vegetable Special

Butternut Squash and Blue Cheese

Vegetarian Tostada

Middle Eastern with Hummus, Feta, and Black Olives

The Vegetarian Special

Bruschetta-Style Pomodoro
with Melted Parmesan

MAKES 1 6-INCH PIZZA (*serves 1*) *or* 1 12-INCH PIZZA (*serves 4–6*)

Among the most popular appetizers in Italian restaurants is bruschetta—slices of crisp grilled bread topped with a simple, aromatic tomato salad. The concept translates perfectly to prebaked pizza crusts. Melting some cheese on the crust before adding the salad elevates it a notch. You can substitute fresh goat cheese, mozzarella, or fontina for the Parmesan, if you wish. If you'd like something more elaborate, put some pesto on the crust before you add the cheese.

Prebaked pizza crust	6-inch	12-inch
Block Parmesan cheese	2 ounces	½ pound
Balsamic vinegar	½ tablespoon	2 tablespoons
Salt and white pepper to taste		
Extra-virgin olive oil	1½ tablespoons	6 tablespoons
Firm, ripe Roma tomatoes	2	8
Small garlic clove, chopped fine	1	4
Fresh basil, shredded fine	1 teaspoon	4 teaspoons
Fresh parsley, chopped fine	1 teaspoon	4 teaspoons

Preheat the oven to 450°F. Place the pizza crust on a baking sheet.

With a cheese shaver or a swivel-bladed vegetable peeler, cut the Parmesan into wide, thin shavings. Arrange them on top of the pizza crust.

Bake until the crust is crisp and the cheese has just begun to brown, about 10 minutes.

While the pizza is baking, prepare the tomato salad. In a bowl, stir together the vinegar, salt, and white pepper. Stir in the olive oil. Add the tomatoes, garlic, basil, and parsley and toss well.

Remove the pizza crust from the oven, transfer to a cutting board, and cut into slices. Spoon the tomato salad on top of the pizza.

Cherry Tomatoes and Pesto

MAKES 1 6-INCH PIZZA (*serves 1*) *or* 1 12-INCH PIZZA (*serves 4–6*)

A great, sweet pleasure of summer, juicy cherry tomatoes star in this easy pizza. If you can find yellow cherry tomatoes, all the better; substitute them for half of the red ones, making an alternating pattern of red and yellow tomato halves.

Prebaked pizza crust	6-inch	12-inch
Pesto sauce	3 tablespoons	¾ cup
Cherry tomatoes, cut in half	10	40
Ricotta cheese	1 ounce	¼ pound
Shredded fontina cheese	1 ounce	¼ pound
Shredded mozzarella cheese	1 ounce	¼ pound
Fresh parsley, chopped fine	½ tablespoon	2 tablespoons

Preheat the oven to 450°F. Place the pizza crust on a baking sheet.

Spread the pesto sauce on top of the crust up to ½ inch from its edge. Arrange the tomatoes on top, alternating them cut sides up and down. Dot with the ricotta and spread evenly with the fontina and mozzarella.

Bake the pizza until the cheese is bubbly and just beginning to brown, about 10 minutes. Remove from the oven, transfer to a cutting board, garnish with parsley, and cut into slices.

Sun-Dried Tomatoes with Ricotta

MAKES 1 6-INCH PIZZA *(serves 1)* or 1 12-INCH PIZZA *(serves 4–6)*

Sun-dried tomatoes have such an intense flavor that you can use them without a sauce—provided, of course, there's another source of moistness, such as the glistening cream and the fluffy ricotta cheese in this recipe.

Prebaked pizza crust	*6-inch*	*12-inch*
Heavy cream	*2 tablespoons*	*½ cup*
Freshly grated Parmesan cheese	*1 tablespoon*	*¼ cup*
Pieces oil-packed sun-dried tomato, cut into thin strips	*4*	*16*
Ricotta cheese	*2 ounces*	*½ pound*
Shredded fontina cheese	*1 ounce*	*¼ pound*
Fresh basil, shredded fine	*½ tablespoon*	*2 tablespoons*

Preheat the oven to 450°F. Place the pizza crust on a baking sheet.

Brush the cream on top of the crust up to ½ inch from its edge and sprinkle evenly with Parmesan. Arrange the sun-dried tomato strips on top. Dot with the ricotta and spread evenly with the shredded fontina.

Bake the pizza until the cheese has melted and begun to brown slightly, about 10 minutes. Remove from the oven, transfer to a cutting board, garnish with basil, and cut into slices.

Rapid Spicy Tomato Sauté with Mozzarella

MAKES 1 6-INCH PIZZA (*serves 1*) *or* 1 12-INCH PIZZA (*serves 4–6*)

In this recipe, you essentially make your own quick pizza sauce from scratch with flavorful summer tomatoes. Add shredded mozzarella and you have an utterly simple, delicious pizza. Leave out the red pepper flakes if you prefer a milder taste.

Prebaked pizza crust	6-inch	12-inch
Extra-virgin olive oil	1 tablespoon	¼ cup
Small garlic clove, chopped fine	1	4
Crushed red pepper flakes	⅛ teaspoon	½ teaspoon
Firm, ripe Roma tomatoes, chopped coarse	2	8
Fresh basil, shredded fine	1 teaspoon	4 teaspoons
Fresh parsley, chopped fine	1 teaspoon	4 teaspoons
Sugar	¼ teaspoon	1 teaspoon
Salt and pepper to taste		
Shredded mozzarella cheese	2 ounces	½ pound

Preheat the oven to 450°F. Place the pizza crust on a baking sheet.

In a frying pan, heat the oil with the garlic and red pepper flakes over medium heat. When the garlic begins to sizzle, add the tomatoes and stir in the basil, parsley, and sugar. Raise the heat slightly and sauté until the juices have almost evaporated, yielding a thick but still slightly liquid sauce. Season to taste with salt and pepper.

Spread the tomato sauce on top of the crust up to ½ inch from its edge. Spread evenly with the mozzarella.

Bake the pizza until the cheese is bubbly and just beginning to brown, about 10 minutes. Remove from the oven, transfer to a cutting board, and cut into slices.

Roasted Peppers with Pesto and Ricotta

MAKES 1 6-INCH PIZZA (*serves 1*) *or* 1 12-INCH PIZZA (*serves 4–6*)

Bottled Italian-style roasted bell peppers work perfectly in this simple pizza, and their sweetness is complemented by that of the ricotta cheese. Look for bottles that include more than one color of pepper, allowing you to make a pattern of red and yellow strips atop the pizza. Try supplementing the peppers with some pitted and halved marinated black olives; or add some very thinly sliced red sweet onions. If you like something a little more substantial, scatter some chunks of canned tuna over the vegetables. Feel free to use pizza sauce instead of the pesto.

Prebaked pizza crust	6-inch	12-inch
Pesto sauce	3 tablespoons	¾ cup
Roasted red bell pepper	1	4
Ricotta cheese	2 ounces	½ pound
Shredded mozzarella cheese	1 ounce	¼ pound
Fresh basil, shredded fine	½ tablespoon	2 tablespoons

Preheat the oven to 450°F. Place the pizza crust on a baking sheet.

Spread the pesto sauce on top of the crust up to ½ inch from its edge. Tear the roasted pepper into thin strips and arrange them on top of the sauce. Dot with the ricotta and spread evenly with the shredded mozzarella.

Bake the pizza until the cheese has melted and begun to brown slightly, about 10 minutes. Remove from the oven, transfer to a cutting board, garnish with basil, and cut into slices.

Crisp Bell Pepper Medley with Fontina and Smoked Mozzarella

MAKES 1 6-INCH PIZZA (*serves 1*) *or* 1 12-INCH PIZZA (*serves 4–6*)

The widespread availability of bell peppers in an array of colors inspired this quick pizza. It makes the most of the peppers' lively crunch and natural sweetness. If the selection is limited, you can of course make the pizza with just one kind of pepper.

Prebaked pizza crust	6-inch	12-inch
Pizza sauce	3 tablespoons	¾ cup
Medium-sized green bell pepper	¼	1
Medium-sized red bell pepper	¼	1
Medium-sized yellow bell pepper	¼	1
Shredded fontina cheese	1½ ounces	6 ounces
Shredded smoked mozzarella cheese	1½ ounces	6 ounces
Fresh basil, shredded fine	½ tablespoon	2 tablespoons

Preheat the oven to 450°F. Place the pizza crust on a baking sheet.

Spread the pizza sauce on top of the crust up to ½ inch from its edge.

Stem and seed the peppers, cutting whole peppers into quarters. Cut crosswise into thin strips. Arrange the strips on top of the sauce in a pattern that pleases you. Spread evenly with the fontina and smoked mozzarella.

Bake the pizza until the cheese has melted and begun to brown slightly, about 10 minutes. Remove from the oven, transfer to a cutting board, garnish with basil, and cut into slices.

Roasted Garlic

MAKES 1 6-INCH PIZZA (*serves 1*) *or* 1 12-INCH PIZZA (*serves 4–6*)

A true garlic lover's pizza, this can be made with your own homemade roasted garlic (see Index) or the store-bought product. Whichever you use, bear in mind that roasting makes garlic's distinctive flavor mellower and sweeter, but nonetheless garlicky! If the roasted garlic has been stored in olive oil, use some of that oil for brushing the crust. Try varying the cheeses; fresh goat cheese, for example, makes an excellent substitution, and a few dabs of ricotta are also very nice. You can spice up the pizza with a light sprinkling of crushed red pepper flakes or a few dashes of hot pepper sauce such as Tabasco.

Prebaked pizza crust	*6-inch*	*12-inch*
Extra-virgin olive oil	*1 tablespoon*	*¼ cup*
Roasted garlic cloves	*4*	*16*
Freshly grated Parmesan cheese	*1 tablespoon*	*¼ cup*
Shredded fontina cheese	*1½ ounces*	*6 ounces*
Shredded mozzarella cheese	*1½ ounces*	*6 ounces*
Fresh basil, shredded fine	*½ tablespoon*	*2 tablespoons*

Preheat the oven to 450°F. Place the pizza crust on a baking sheet.

With a basting brush, coat the pizza crust with the olive oil up to ½ inch from its edge. Mash the roasted garlic cloves on the crust, spreading them evenly. Sprinkle with Parmesan and spread evenly with the fontina and mozzarella.

Bake the pizza until the cheese is melted and just beginning to brown, about 10 minutes. Remove from the oven, garnish with basil, and cut into slices.

Garlic-Mushroom Sauté with Fontina

MAKES 1 6-INCH PIZZA (*serves 1*) *or* 1 12-INCH PIZZA (*serves 4–6*)

Mushrooms and garlic go so well together. Add cheese and a bread base, and you have a perfectly simple pizza. The recipe below calls for ordinary cultivated mushrooms of the sort you find in your supermarket. Feel free to substitute any other fresh mushrooms that present themselves in the market—cremini, portobello, chanterelles, shiitakes, and so on—for all or part of the regular ones.

Prebaked pizza crust	6-inch	12-inch
Extra-virgin olive oil	2 tablespoons	½ cup
Large garlic clove, chopped fine	1	4
Fresh mushrooms, sliced thick	2 ounces	½ pound
Fresh chives, chopped fine	1 teaspoon	4 teaspoons
Fresh parsley, chopped fine	1 teaspoon	4 teaspoons
Freshly ground black pepper to taste		
Freshly grated Parmesan cheese	1 tablespoon	¼ cup
Shredded fontina cheese	3 ounces	¾ pound

Preheat the oven to 450°F. Place the pizza crust on a baking sheet.

In a frying pan large enough to hold the sliced mushrooms comfortably in a single layer, heat the oil with the garlic over high heat. As soon as the garlic sizzles, add the mushrooms and sauté until their edges begin to turn golden, 3 to 4 minutes. Stir in the chives and parsley and remove from the heat.

Spread the mushrooms and their juices on top of the crust up to ½ inch from its edge. Season lightly with black pepper. Sprinkle evenly with the Parmesan and then with the fontina.

Bake the pizza until the cheese is melted and just beginning to brown, about 10 minutes. Remove from the oven, transfer to a cutting board, and cut into slices.

Asparagus Parmigiana

MAKES 1 6-INCH PIZZA (*serves 1*) *or* 1 12-INCH PIZZA (*serves 4–6*)

Buy a good-quality block Parmesan for this simple pizza, which highlights springtime's best asparagus. The olive oil–Parmesan treatment also works well with other vegetables. Try substituting quickly grilled thin slices of Japanese eggplant, strips of sun-dried tomato, roasted bell peppers, thinly sliced mushrooms, or raw baby spinach leaves.

Prebaked pizza crust	6-inch	12-inch
Medium-sized spears asparagus	4	16
Extra-virgin olive oil	2 tablespoons	½ cup
Block Parmesan cheese	2 ounces	½ pound
Freshly ground black pepper to taste		

Preheat the oven to 450°F. Place the pizza crust on a baking sheet.

While the oven is preheating, bring a medium saucepan of salted water to a boil. Trim the tough ends of the asparagus spears; then cut the asparagus diagonally into ¼-inch-thick slices, leaving the tender tips intact. Parboil the asparagus, tips included, for 30 seconds; immediately drain, rinse under cold running water, and drain again.

Spread the olive oil on top of the crust up to ½ inch from its edge. With a cheese shaver or a swivel-bladed vegetable peeler, cut the Parmesan into wide, thin shavings. Distribute about a quarter of them on top of the olive oil. Arrange the asparagus pieces on top, then cover with the remaining Parmesan shavings.

Bake the pizza until the cheese has melted, about 10 minutes. Remove from the oven, transfer to a cutting board, season to taste with black pepper, and cut into slices.

Charred Eggplant
with Mozzarella and Basil

MAKES 1 6-INCH PIZZA (*serves 1*) *or* 1 12-INCH PIZZA (*serves 4–6*)

Charbroiling gives eggplant a wonderfully smoky edge to complement its sweet, earthy flavor. Instead of taking the time to fire up the charcoal grill, use a ridged stovetop grill pan to cook the vegetable. Long, slender Japanese eggplants, now widely available in well-stocked greengrocers and supermarket produce sections, have a finer flavor and texture, with none of the bitterness that requires the advance salting and draining of larger globe eggplants. Pesto sauce may be substituted for the pizza sauce, and a little fresh, creamy goat cheese makes a nice addition.

Prebaked pizza crust	*6-inch*	*12-inch*
Pizza sauce	*3 tablespoons*	*¾ cup*
Japanese eggplant	*1*	*4*
Extra-virgin olive oil	*1 tablespoon*	*¼ cup*
Salt and black pepper to taste		
Shredded mozzarella cheese	*3 ounces*	*¾ pound*
Fresh basil, shredded fine	*½ tablespoon*	*2 tablespoons*

Preheat the oven to 450°F. Place the pizza crust on a baking sheet.

Spread the pizza sauce on top of the crust up to ½ inch from its edge.

Trim the eggplant; then use the tip of a small sharp knife to score its skin lengthwise two or three times. Cut the eggplant crosswise into ¼-inch-thick slices. With a small basting brush, brush the slices lightly with the olive oil and sprinkle them to taste with salt and black pepper.

Heat a stovetop grill pan over medium-high heat. Add the eggplant slices and cook until lightly charred, 1 to 2 minutes per side.

Arrange the eggplant slices overlapping on top of the pizza sauce. Spread the mozzarella evenly on top.

Bake the pizza until the cheese has melted and begun to brown slightly, about 10 minutes. Remove from the oven, transfer to a cutting board, garnish with basil, and cut into slices.

Texas-Style Grilled Corn

MAKES 1 6-INCH PIZZA (*serves 1*) *or* 1 12-INCH PIZZA (*serves 4–6*)

This great vegetarian pizza is full of lively Southwestern flavors. If you want an even punchier result, add a little finely chopped jalapeño chili along with the mild green chilies. You could also make this with regular pizza sauce.

Prebaked pizza crust	6-inch	12-inch
Barbecue sauce	3 tablespoons	¾ cup
Ear fresh sweet corn, husk and silk removed	½	2
Unsalted butter, melted	½ tablespoon	2 tablespoons
Salt and white pepper to taste		
Canned chopped mild green chilies	1 tablespoon	¼ cup
Shredded Monterey Jack cheese	2 ounces	½ pound
Shredded cheddar cheese	1 ounce	¼ pound
Cilantro, chopped fine	½ tablespoon	2 tablespoons

Preheat the oven to 450°F. Place the pizza crust on a baking sheet. Spread the barbecue sauce on top of the crust up to ½ inch from its edge.

Meanwhile, bring a saucepan of water to a boil. Add the corn and boil for 3 minutes. Drain well and pat the corn dry with paper towels.

Using a heavy, preferably cast-iron, frying pan, melt the butter over medium-high heat. Brush the corn with the melted butter and sprinkle to taste with salt and white pepper. Cook the corn in the skillet, turning the ears carefully with tongs, until lightly scorched on all sides, 2 to 4 minutes. Remove from the pan and, when cool enough to handle, carefully cut the kernels from the ears with a sharp knife.

Sprinkle the corn kernels evenly over the barbecue sauce. Scatter the chilies on top and sprinkle the Monterey Jack and cheddar evenly over the pizza.

Bake the pizza until the cheese is melted and just beginning to brown, about 10 minutes. Remove from the oven, transfer to a cutting board, garnish with cilantro, and cut into slices.

Four Seasons

MAKES 1 6-INCH PIZZA (*serves 1*) *or* 1 12-INCH PIZZA (*serves 4–6*)

Though modern agriculture and airfreight make a wide range of vegetables available year-round, each of those that tops this traditional pizza is believed to represent an individual season: mushrooms for autumn, carrots for winter, asparagus for spring, and tomatoes for summer. Let seasonal availability dictate any changes you might make. You can substitute pesto for the pizza sauce.

Prebaked pizza crust	*6-inch*	*12-inch*
Pizza sauce	3 tablespoons	¾ cup
Freshly grated Parmesan cheese	1 tablespoon	¼ cup
Medium-sized cultivated mushrooms, sliced thin	2	8
Thin stalk asparagus, sliced thin	1	4
Shredded carrot	2 tablespoons	½ cup
Firm, ripe Roma tomato, sliced thin	½	2
Shredded fontina cheese	1½ ounces	6 ounces
Shredded mozzarella cheese	1½ ounces	6 ounces
Fresh basil, shredded fine	1 teaspoon	4 teaspoons
Fresh parsley, chopped fine	1 teaspoon	4 teaspoons

Preheat the oven to 450°F. Place the pizza crust on a baking sheet.

Spread the pizza sauce on the crust up to ½ inch from its edge. Sprinkle with Parmesan. Arrange each of the vegetables on top of the sauce on one fourth of the pizza. Spread evenly with the fontina and mozzarella.

Bake the pizza until the cheese is melted and just beginning to brown, about 10 minutes. Remove from the oven, garnish with basil and parsley, and cut into slices.

Roasted Vegetables
with Extra-Virgin Olive Oil

MAKES 1 6-INCH PIZZA (*serves 1*) *or* 1 12-INCH PIZZA (*serves 4–6*)

A pizza perfectly suited to the diet-conscious who want pizza without the cheese, this features a selection of fresh vegetables, uncovered by cheese and sliced so thinly that they roast during their brief exposure to the oven's heat. If you wish, you can add a light smear of pizza or pesto sauce to the crust before arranging the vegetables, rub it with a cut half of a garlic clove, or spread it with roasted garlic. Feel free to add any other seasonal vegetables you like that can be sliced thin and arranged neatly.

Prebaked pizza crust	*6-inch*	*12-inch*
Medium-sized cultivated mushrooms	*2*	*8*
Small carrot	*½*	*2*
Small Japanese eggplant	*½*	*2*
Small zucchini	*½*	*2*
Small red onion	*¼*	*1*
Extra-virgin olive oil	*1 tablespoon*	*¼ cup*
Salt to taste		
Dried oregano	*¼ teaspoon*	*1 teaspoon*
Fresh basil, shredded fine	*½ tablespoon*	*2 tablespoons*

Preheat the oven to 450°F. Place the pizza crust on a baking sheet.

Cut all the vegetables crosswise into thin slices, no more than about ⅛ inch thick.

With a basting brush, coat the pizza crust with half of the olive oil, up to ½ inch from its edge. Arrange the vegetables on top in an attractive pattern, giving each its own segment of the pizza or mixing them as you like. Brush with the remaining oil, sprinkle with salt, and then, with your fingertips, crumble the oregano over the vegetables.

Bake the pizza until the crust is crisp and the vegetables are just beginning to turn golden, about 10 minutes. Remove from the oven, garnish with basil, and cut into slices.

Spinach Salad
with Garlic-Herb Cream Cheese

MAKES 1 6-INCH PIZZA (*serves 1*) *or* 1 12-INCH PIZZA (*serves 4–6*)

This recipe offers a simple pizza covered in rich, aromatic cheese and topped with a salad of fresh spinach leaves tossed with a lemony dressing. If you wish, you can crumble some crisp bacon into the spinach before tossing. It's a good idea to eat this pizza with a fork and knife.

Prebaked pizza crust	*6-inch*	*12-inch*
Garlic-herb cream cheese, at room temperature	*3 ounces*	*¾ pound*
Packed spinach leaves	*¾ cup*	*3 cups*
Lemon juice	*½ tablespoon*	*2 tablespoons*
Creamy Dijon-style mustard	*½ teaspoon*	*2 teaspoons*
Sugar	*¼ teaspoon*	*1 teaspoon*
Salt and white pepper to taste		
Extra-virgin olive oil	*1½ tablespoons*	*6 tablespoons*

Preheat the oven to 450°F. Place the pizza crust on a baking sheet.

Spread the garlic-herb cream cheese on top of the crust up to ½ inch from its edge. Bake the pizza until the cheese is bubbly, about 10 minutes.

While the pizza bakes, prepare the spinach salad. Thoroughly wash and dry the leaves, then stack them and cut crosswise into ¼- to-½-inch shreds. In a small bowl, stir together the lemon juice, mustard, sugar, salt, and white pepper to taste. Whisking continuously, slowly pour in the olive oil. In a mixing bowl, toss the spinach with enough dressing to coat it to your liking.

Remove the pizza from the oven, transfer to a cutting board, top with the spinach salad, and cut into slices.

Arugula and Goat Cheese

MAKES 1 6-INCH PIZZA (*serves 1*) *or* 1 12-INCH PIZZA (*serves 4–6*)

The refreshing bitterness of bright green arugula leaves, also called rocket, finds a rich, tangy complement in fresh, creamy goat cheese. You'll find both in well-stocked supermarkets. Seek out the excellent goat cheeses being made in northern California's wine country, which can be particularly mild, sweet, and rich. You could substitute shredded radicchio or Belgian endive for the arugula, and a commercial garlic-herb cream cheese for the goat cheese.

Prebaked pizza crust	6-inch	12-inch
Fresh creamy goat cheese, at room temperature	3 ounces	¾ pound
Freshly ground black pepper to taste		
Packed arugula leaves	½ cup	2 cups
Salt to taste		
Extra-virgin olive oil	1 ½ tablespoons	6 tablespoons

Preheat the oven to 450°F. Place the pizza crust on a baking sheet.

Spread half of the goat cheese on top of the crust up to ½ inch from its edge.

Sprinkle lightly with black pepper. Arrange the arugula leaves on top, pressing them down gently into the cheese. Sprinkle lightly with salt, dot with the remaining cheese, and drizzle with olive oil.

Bake the pizza until the arugula has wilted and the goat cheese has melted, about 10 minutes. Remove from the oven, transfer to a cutting board, and cut into slices.

Marinated Artichokes with Sun-Dried Tomatoes and Fontina

MAKES 1 6-INCH PIZZA (*serves 1*) or 1 12-INCH PIZZA (*serves 4–6*)

Though the combination seems very much a salute to California cuisine, the featured ingredients in fact look toward the Mediterranean. If you like, you can add pitted marinated black olives and substitute creamy goat cheese for some or all of the fontina. Pizza sauce can be used in place of the pesto sauce; or use a 50–50 combination, swirling them together.

Prebaked pizza crust	*6-inch*	*12-inch*
Pesto sauce	3 tablespoons	¾ cup
Marinated artichoke hearts, drained	¼ cup	1 cup
Oil-packed sun-dried tomatoes, drained	¼ cup	1 cup
Shredded fontina cheese	2 ounces	½ pound
Shredded mozzarella cheese	1 ounce	¼ pound
Dried oregano	¼ teaspoon	1 teaspoon

Preheat the oven to 450°F. Place the pizza crust on a baking sheet.

Spread the pesto sauce on top of the crust up to ½ inch from its edge.

Cut the artichoke hearts and sun-dried tomatoes into ¼-inch-thick slices and scatter them on top of the sauce. Sprinkle evenly with the fontina and mozzarella. With your fingertips, crumble the oregano over the cheese.

Bake the pizza until the cheeses have melted, about 10 minutes. Remove from the oven, transfer to a cutting board, and cut into slices.

Marinated Vegetable Special

MAKES 1 6-INCH PIZZA (*serves 1*) or 1 12-INCH PIZZA (*serves 4–6*)

Any well-stocked supermarket will carry a wide array of marinated vegetables—many of them Italian imports or Italian-style—ready to top a quick pizza with distinction. This recipe shows off a variety of them, their bold flavors subtly muted by ricotta and mozzarella cheeses. Oil-packed sun-dried tomatoes make a nice addition. If you like anchovies, add a few to the topping, too. Pesto would work equally well for the sauce; or you could even prepare this as a sauceless pizza.

Prebaked pizza crust	6-inch	12-inch
Pizza sauce	3 tablespoons	¾ cup
Pieces marinated artichoke hearts, sliced thin	2	8
Marinated mushrooms, sliced thin	2	8
Heart of palm, sliced thin	1	4
Roasted marinated red bell pepper, torn into strips	½	2
Marinated black olives, pitted and halved	4	16
Ricotta cheese	1½ ounces	6 ounces
Shredded mozzarella cheese	1½ ounces	6 ounces
Fresh basil, shredded fine	½ tablespoon	2 tablespoons

Preheat the oven to 450°F. Place the pizza crust on a baking sheet.

Spread the pizza sauce on top of the crust up to ½ inch from its edge. Arrange the vegetables on top in a pattern of your choosing. Dot the vegetables with the ricotta and spread evenly with the mozzarella.

Bake the pizza until the cheese is bubbly and just beginning to brown, about 10 minutes. Remove from the oven, transfer to a cutting board, garnish with basil, and cut into slices.

Butternut Squash and Blue Cheese

MAKES 1 6-INCH PIZZA (*serves 1*) *or* 1 12-INCH PIZZA (*serves 4–6*)

It may sound like an odd combination, but the subtle sweetness of orange-fleshed winter squash and the sharp tang of blue cheese go together very well. The quick pizza's brief baking cooks the squash slightly, leaving it with a pleasant edge of crispness. You could substitute any other hard-shelled winter squash, such as buttercup, acorn, hubbard, or turban. To shred the squash, carefully use a large, sharp knife to cut it in quarters. Scrape out the seeds with a sturdy spoon. Carefully cut off the hard outer shell. Then shred on the large holes of a box grater or in a food processor fitted with a shredding disk.

Prebaked pizza crust	6-inch	12-inch
Shredded butternut squash	½ cup	2 cups
Extra-virgin olive oil	1 tablespoon	¼ cup
Unsalted butter, melted	1 tablespoon	¼ cup
Fresh chives, chopped fine	½ tablespoon	2 tablespoons
Fresh parsley, chopped fine	½ tablespoon	2 tablespoons
Small garlic clove, chopped fine (optional)	1	4
Salt and pepper to taste		
Blue cheese, crumbled	2 ounces	½ pound
Shredded mozzarella cheese	1 ounce	¼ pound

Preheat the oven to 450°F. Place the pizza crust on a baking sheet.

In a mixing bowl, toss together the squash, olive oil, butter, chives, parsley, garlic, and salt and pepper to taste. Add half the crumbled blue cheese and toss again.

Spread the squash mixture evenly on top of the pizza crust up to ½ inch from its edge. Sprinkle with the remaining blue cheese and spread the mozzarella on top.

Bake the pizza until the cheese is melted and just beginning to brown, about 10 minutes. Remove from the oven and cut into slices.

Vegetarian Tostada

MAKES 1 6-INCH PIZZA *(serves 1)* or 1 12-INCH PIZZA *(serves 4–6)*

Canned refried beans, which are generally of excellent quality, make this quick Mexican-style pizza a snap. I'm especially fond of some of the new fat-free seasoned varieties now available, which can become the basis for a very healthy version of this recipe using reduced-fat cheese and fat-free sour cream. Most well-stocked supermarkets also carry ready-made fresh salsas in their refrigerated cases.

Prebaked pizza crust	*6-inch*	*12-inch*
Canned refried beans	*½ cup*	*2 cups*
Canned chopped mild green chilies	*1 tablespoon*	*¼ cup*
Shredded Monterey Jack cheese	*1½ ounces*	*6 ounces*
Shredded cheddar cheese	*1½ ounces*	*6 ounces*
Iceberg lettuce leaf, shredded fine	*1*	*4*
Fresh tomato salsa	*2 tablespoons*	*½ cup*
Sliced, pitted black olives	*1 tablespoon*	*¼ cup*
Sour cream	*1 tablespoon*	*¼ cup*
Avocado, peeled, pitted, and sliced thin	*¼*	*1*

Preheat the oven to 450°F. Place the pizza crust on a baking sheet.

Spread the refried beans on top of the crust up to ½ inch from its edge. Sprinkle evenly with the chilies; then spread the Monterey Jack and cheddar on top.

Bake the pizza until the cheese has melted and begun to brown slightly, about 10 minutes. Remove from the oven and cut into slices. Garnish to taste with the remaining ingredients.

Middle Eastern with Hummus, Feta, and Black Olives

MAKES 1 6-INCH PIZZA (*serves 1*) *or* 1 12-INCH PIZZA (*serves 4–6*)

Hummus, a rich-tasting chickpea puree usually served with hot triangles of pita bread, works perfectly as a quick pizza topping—especially when a little cheese has been melted first on top of the crust. Even if you're planning on topping a small 6-inch crust, you might consider making the larger quantity of hummus. Keep the extra dip covered in the refrigerator for later use as a delicious snack or appetizer.

Prebaked pizza crust	*6-inch*	*12-inch*
Feta cheese	*1 ½ ounces*	*6 ounces*
Shredded mozzarella cheese	*1 ½ ounces*	*6 ounces*
Canned chickpeas (garbanzo beans), drained	*½ cup*	*2 cups*
Tahini (sesame seed paste)	*1 tablespoon*	*¼ cup*
Lemon juice	*½ tablespoon*	*2 tablespoons*
Small garlic clove, chopped fine	*1*	*4*
Extra-virgin olive oil	*1 tablespoon*	*¼ cup*
Salt and white pepper to taste		
Fresh parsley, chopped fine	*½ tablespoon*	*2 tablespoons*
Marinated black olives, pitted and halved	*6*	*24*

Preheat the oven to 450°F. Place the pizza crust on a baking sheet.

Crumble the feta evenly over the crust up to ½ inch from its edge. Sprinkle the mozzarella evenly on top.

Bake the pizza until the cheese has melted and begun to brown slightly, about 10 minutes.

While the pizza bakes, prepare the hummus. Put the chickpeas, tahini, lemon juice, and garlic in a food processor fitted with the metal blade. Pulse several times; then process until smoothly pureed, stopping once or twice to scrape down the bowl. Pulse in up to half of the olive oil to achieve a smoother consistency. Then pulse in salt and white pepper to taste.

Remove the pizza from the oven and spread it with the hummus. Scatter the parsley and distribute the olives on top. Drizzle with the remaining olive oil. Cut into slices.

The Vegetarian Special

MAKES 1 6-INCH PIZZA (*serves 1*) *or* 1 12-INCH PIZZA (*serves 4–6*)

I remember a time not so long ago when any trendy café or health-food restaurant would offer a sandwich filled with just the sort of ingredients that top this pizza. Though the combination seems kind of quaint now, it's still surprisingly good. Add any elaborations that your own memories suggest.

Prebaked pizza crust	*6-inch*	*12-inch*
Grainy mustard	1 tablespoon	¼ cup
Mayonnaise	1 tablespoon	¼ cup
Muenster cheese, sliced thin	1 ounce	¼ pound
Monterey Jack cheese, sliced thin	1 ounce	¼ pound
Medium-sized ripe avocado	¼	1
Lemon juice	½ teaspoon	2 teaspoons
Salt and white pepper to taste		
Shelled, toasted sunflower seeds	1 tablespoon	¼ cup
Firm, ripe Roma tomato, sliced thin	1	4
Alfalfa or mustard sprouts	2 tablespoons	½ cup

Preheat the oven to 450°F. Place the pizza crust on a baking sheet.

In a small bowl, stir together the mustard and mayonnaise and spread the mixture on top of the crust up to ½ inch from its edge. Arrange the Muenster and Monterey Jack slices evenly on top.

Bake the pizza until the cheese is bubbly and just beginning to brown, about 10 minutes.

While the pizza is baking, peel and pit the avocado and mash it with the lemon juice and salt and white pepper to taste.

Remove the pizza from the oven and transfer to a cutting board. Spread it evenly with the mashed avocado and sprinkle with sunflower seeds. Arrange the tomato slices on top and season them to taste with a little salt. Garnish with sprouts and cut into slices.

CHAPTER SIX

Cheese and Egg Toppings

Classic Four-Cheese

Fresh Mozzarella and Summer Tomato

Mozzarella and Pesto

Smoked Mozzarella with Pesto and Sun-Dried Tomatoes

Ploughman's Lunch

Swiss-Style Raclette with Diced Potato, Cornichons, and Grainy Mustard

Gorgonzola and Pine Nuts with Mascarpone

Gorgonzola and Tomato

Gorgonzola and Pear with Mascarpone and Almonds

Roquefort and Red Flame Grapes

Fresh Goat Cheese and Herbs

Goat Cheese and Garlic with Extra-Virgin Olive Oil

Liptauer

Ricotta Soufflé

Baked Egg with Tomato and Pesto Sauces and Smoked Mozzarella

Scrambled Egg with Garlic-Herb Cream Cheese

Lox, Egg, and Onion

Scrambled Egg and Bacon with Smoked Cheddar

Scrambled Egg with Sun-Dried Tomatoes and Shaved Parmesan

Scrambled Egg Whites with Smoked Turkey and Light Cheeses

Classic Four-Cheese

MAKES 1 6-INCH PIZZA *(serves 1)* or 1 12-INCH PIZZA *(serves 4–6)*

For a change of pace, try arranging each of the four cheeses separately over one fourth of the pizza's surface. Substitute pesto sauce for the pizza sauce, if you like. Pitted brine-cured black olives such as French Niçoise or Italian Gaeta make a nice garnish.

Prebaked pizza crust	6-inch	12-inch
Pizza sauce	3 tablespoons	¾ cup
Freshly grated Parmesan cheese	1 tablespoon	¼ cup
Blue cheese	½ ounce	2 ounces
Fontina cheese	½ ounce	2 ounces
Shredded mozzarella cheese	1 ounce	¼ pound
Dried oregano	¼ teaspoon	1 teaspoon

Preheat the oven to 450°F. Place the pizza crust on a baking sheet.

Spread the pizza sauce on top of the crust up to ½ inch from its edge. Sprinkle the Parmesan evenly over the sauce. Crumble the blue cheese and dot the fontina cheese on top. Finish with a layer of mozzarella. With your fingertips, crumble the oregano evenly over the cheeses.

Bake the pizza until the cheeses are bubbly and just beginning to brown, about 10 minutes. Remove from the oven, transfer to a cutting board, and cut into slices.

Fresh Mozzarella and Summer Tomato

MAKES 1 6-INCH PIZZA (*serves 1*) *or* 1 12-INCH PIZZA (*serves 4–6*)

Look for fresh mozzarella in Italian delicatessens or well-stocked food stores; you can, if you must, substitute packaged mozzarella. This pizza will be at its best in summer, when vine-ripened tomatoes are at their peak of flavor; at other times of year, use Roma tomatoes, doubling the tomato quantities given.

Prebaked pizza crust	6-inch	12-inch
Firm, medium-sized vine-ripened tomato	½	2
Salt to taste		
Fresh basil, shredded fine	1 teaspoon	4 teaspoons
Extra-virgin olive oil	1 tablespoon	¼ cup
Fresh mozzarella cheese, drained	3 ounces	¾ pound
Freshly ground black pepper to taste		

Preheat the oven to 450°F. Place the pizza crust on a baking sheet.

With a small sharp knife, core the tomato. Cut crosswise into ¼-inch-thick slices. Arrange the slices on top of the pizza crust. Sprinkle with salt to taste, scatter with basil, and drizzle with olive oil.

Cut the mozzarella into ¼-inch-thick slices and arrange them on top of the tomatoes.

Bake until the cheese has melted, about 10 minutes. Remove from the oven and season to taste with pepper. Transfer to a cutting board and cut into slices.

Mozzarella and Pesto

MAKES 1 6-INCH PIZZA (*serves 1*) *or* 1 12-INCH PIZZA (*serves 4–6*)

In its own way, this pizza is as profoundly simple as the basic cheese-and-tomato combination of old. If you feel the urge to elaborate upon it, do so only by substituting fontina for half of the mozzarella.

Prebaked pizza crust	*6-inch*	*12-inch*
Pesto sauce	*3 tablespoons*	*¾ cup*
Shredded mozzarella cheese	*3 ounces*	*¾ pound*
Fresh basil, shredded fine	*½ tablespoon*	*2 tablespoons*

Preheat the oven to 450°F. Place the pizza crust on a baking sheet.

Spread the pesto on top of the crust up to ½ inch from its edge. Sprinkle evenly with the mozzarella.

Bake the pizza until the cheese is melted and just beginning to brown, about 10 minutes. Remove from the oven, transfer to a cutting board, garnish with basil, and cut into slices.

Smoked Mozzarella with Pesto and Sun-Dried Tomatoes

MAKES 1 6-INCH PIZZA (*serves 1*) or 1 12-INCH PIZZA (*serves 4–6*)

An intense combination of flavors and colors, this pizza is utter simplicity to make. I like to cut the mozzarella into thin slices; but you can use shredded if you like.

Prebaked pizza crust	6-inch	12-inch
Pesto sauce	3 tablespoons	¾ cup
Pieces oil-packed sun-dried tomatoes, drained	3	12
Smoked mozzarella cheese, sliced thin	3 ounces	¾ pound
Fresh parsley, chopped fine	1 teaspoon	4 teaspoons

Preheat the oven to 450°F. Place the pizza crust on a baking sheet.

Spread the pesto on top of the crust up to ½ inch from its edge. Using kitchen scissors or a sharp knife, cut the sun-dried tomatoes into thin strips and scatter them evenly over the sauce. Place the smoked mozzarella slices on top.

Bake the pizza until the cheese is melted and just beginning to brown, about 10 minutes. Remove from the oven, transfer to a cutting board, garnish with parsley, and cut into slices.

Ploughman's Lunch

MAKES 1 6-INCH PIZZA (*serves 1*) *or* 1 12-INCH PIZZA (*serves 4–6*)

Throughout Britain the ploughman's lunch is a time-honored pub meal consisting of a chunk of good local cheese, a generous dollop of Branston pickle or chutney, and a hunk of bread. Sounds to me like a formula for a quick, flavorful pizza. A note of caution: English mustard is powerful, sinus-clearing stuff, and if it's not to your liking you can substitute creamy Dijon-style mustard. Fruit chutneys tend to be subtly spiced, and I like those on the sweeter side, my favorite being mango chutney. In most brands, the mango pieces can be fairly large and should be cut into thin strips before the chutney is spread on the crust.

Prebaked pizza crust	6-inch	12-inch
Prepared English mustard	½ teaspoon	2 teaspoons
Fruit chutney or Branston pickle	2 tablespoons	½ cup
Shredded sharp cheddar cheese	3 ounces	¾ pound
Fresh chives, chopped fine	½ teaspoon	2 teaspoons

Preheat the oven to 450°F. Place the pizza crust on a baking sheet.

Spread the mustard on top of the crust up to ½ inch from its edge. Spread the chutney on top. Sprinkle evenly with the cheddar.

Bake the pizza until the cheese is melted, about 10 minutes. Remove from the oven, garnish with chives, transfer to a cutting board, and cut into slices.

Swiss-Style Raclette with Diced Potato, Cornichons, and Grainy Mustard

MAKES 1 6-INCH PIZZA (*serves 1*) *or* 1 12-INCH PIZZA (*serves 4–6*)

One of Switzerland's national dishes—in which cheese is melted before an open fire and served with potatoes and pickles—translates beautifully to a quick, savory pizza. True raclette cheese may be hard to find outside Switzerland; but, for this purpose at least, you can substitute Emmentaler, Appenzeller, Gruyère, or any other good-quality Swiss cheese. If you cannot find Yukon Gold potatoes, substitute another good-quality small boiling potato. You'll find jars of French cornichons, tiny pickled sour cucumbers, in well-stocked food stores.

Prebaked pizza crust	*6-inch*	*12-inch*
Yukon Gold potato	*1*	*4*
Grainy mustard	*1½ tablespoons*	*6 tablespoons*
Heavy cream	*½ tablespoon*	*2 tablespoons*
French cornichons, cut into		
¼-inch-thick slices	*4*	*16*
Fresh chives, chopped fine	*½ tablespoon*	*2 tablespoons*
Shredded Swiss cheese	*3 ounces*	*¾ pound*

Preheat the oven to 450°F. Place the pizza crust on a baking sheet.

Cut the potato into quarters, put them in a saucepan, and cover with cold water. Bring to a boil and cook until tender enough to be pierced easily with the tip of a small sharp knife, 10 to 15 minutes. Drain well, rinse with cold water, and drain again. Cut into ½-inch dice.

In a small bowl, stir together the mustard and cream and spread on top of the pizza crust up to ½ inch from its edge. Scatter the potato on top, then the cornichons, and sprinkle with chives. Top with the shredded Swiss cheese.

Bake the pizza until the cheese is bubbly and just beginning to brown, about 10 minutes. Remove from the oven, transfer to a cutting board, and cut into slices.

Gorgonzola and Pine Nuts with Mascarpone

MAKES 1 6-INCH PIZZA (*serves 1*) or 1 12-INCH PIZZA (*serves 4–6*)

Italy's great blue cheese shines in this simple pizza, elaborated by a subtle hint of garlic. Feel free to substitute any other good-quality blue-veined cheese that is available. Likewise, pine nuts—*pignoli* in Italy—could give way to other favorite nuts, such as pecans or almonds, cut into similarly sized pieces. If mascarpone—a thick, slightly soured Italian cream cheese sold at Italian delicatessens and well-stocked supermarkets—is unavailable, simply combine equal parts cream cheese and heavy cream.

Prebaked pizza crust	6-inch	12-inch
Garlic clove, cut in half	1	4
Mascarpone	3 tablespoons	¾ cup
Gorgonzola cheese	3 ounces	¾ pound
Pine nuts	1 tablespoon	¼ cup
Fresh basil, shredded fine	1 teaspoon	1 ½ tablespoons

Preheat the oven to 450°F. Place the pizza crust on a baking sheet.

Lightly rub the top of the pizza crust with the cut edge of the garlic clove. Spread the mascarpone over the crust up to ½ inch from its edge. Crumble the Gorgonzola evenly on top, then scatter with the pine nuts.

Bake the pizza until the cheese is melted, about 10 minutes. Remove from the oven, transfer to a cutting board, garnish with fresh basil, and cut into slices.

Gorgonzola and Tomato

MAKES 1 6-INCH PIZZA (*serves 1*) *or* 1 12-INCH PIZZA (*serves 4–6*)

Powerful though the flavor of a good blue-veined cheese like Gorgonzola is, it finds a surprising complement in the sweetness of tomato. You could substitute another high-quality blue cheese, such as Stilton, Roquefort, or Maytag.

Prebaked pizza crust	6-inch	12-inch
Pizza sauce	1 ½ tablespoons	6 tablespoons
Firm, ripe Roma tomato, sliced thin	1	4
Gorgonzola cheese	2 ounces	½ pound
Shredded fontina cheese	1 ounce	¼ pound
Fresh basil, chopped fine	½ tablespoon	2 tablespoons

Preheat the oven to 450°F. Place the pizza crust on a baking sheet.

Spread the pizza sauce on top of the crust up to ½ inch from its edge. Arrange the tomato slices on top and crumble or dot the Gorgonzola over them. Sprinkle evenly with the fontina.

Bake the pizza until the cheese is melted, about 10 minutes. Remove from the oven, transfer to a cutting board, garnish with basil, and cut into slices.

Gorgonzola and Pear with Mascarpone and Almonds

MAKES 1 6-INCH PIZZA *(serves 1)* or 1 12-INCH PIZZA *(serves 4–6)*

Blue cheese and pears make a classic combination. Choose the ripest sweet pears you can find, such as Bosc, Bartlett, Stark Crimson Red, or d'Anjou. Or try Asian pears, a crisp crossbreed of apples and pears that is appearing in well-stocked markets and produce shops with increasing frequency. Substitute another blue cheese such as Stilton, Roquefort, or Maytag if you can't find Gorgonzola. If you can't find the tangy, fluid Italian cream cheese known as mascarpone, you can make a reasonable facsimile by mashing together equal parts softened cream cheese and heavy cream.

Prebaked pizza crust	*6-inch*	*12-inch*
Mascarpone	*3 tablespoons*	*¾ cup*
Gorgonzola cheese	*2 ounces*	*½ pound*
Medium-sized firm ripe pear	*½*	*2*
Shredded fontina cheese	*1½ ounces*	*6 ounces*

Preheat the oven to 450°F. Place the pizza crust on a baking sheet.

Spread the mascarpone on top of the crust up to ½ inch from its edge. Crumble the Gorgonzola evenly on top.

Halve, peel, and core the pear. Cut lengthwise into thin slices and arrange them evenly on top of the pizza, gently pressing them down. Scatter the fontina on top.

Bake the pizza until the cheese is melted, about 10 minutes. Remove from the oven, transfer to a cutting board, and cut into slices.

Roquefort and Red Flame Grapes

MAKES 1 6-INCH PIZZA (*serves 1*) *or* 1 12-INCH PIZZA (*serves 4–6*)

Roquefort, the great blue cheese of France, is one of the best cheeses to enjoy with fruit, and the wonderful seedless red flame grapes are a perfect complement to its rich, salty tang. Substitute other creamy blue cheeses if you must, and any other sweet seedless grapes.

Prebaked pizza crust	6-inch	12-inch
Roquefort cheese, at room temperature	2 ounces	½ pound
Red flame seedless grapes, cut in half	¼ cup	1 cup
Shredded fontina cheese	1½ ounces	6 ounces

Preheat the oven to 450°F. Place the pizza crust on a baking sheet.

Spread the Roquefort cheese on top of the crust up to ½ inch from its edge. Distribute the grape halves evenly, cut sides down, and press them into the cheese. Scatter the fontina on top.

Bake the pizza until the cheese is melted, about 10 minutes. Remove from the oven, transfer to a cutting board, and cut into slices.

Fresh Goat Cheese and Herbs

MAKES 1 6-INCH PIZZA (*serves 1*) *or* 1 12-INCH PIZZA (*serves 4–6*)

The richness and tang of fresh, creamy goat cheese is highlighted in this simple pizza. You'll find good-quality goat cheese—both imported and excellent domestic products—in well-stocked supermarkets.

Prebaked pizza crust	*6-inch*	*12-inch*
Fresh, creamy goat cheese, softened	*2 ounces*	*½ pound*
Extra-virgin olive oil	*½ tablespoon*	*2 tablespoons*
Fresh basil, chopped fine	*½ teaspoon*	*2 teaspoons*
Fresh chives, chopped fine	*½ teaspoon*	*2 teaspoons*
Fresh parsley, chopped fine	*½ teaspoon*	*2 teaspoons*
Shredded mozzarella cheese	*2 ounces*	*½ pound*

Preheat the oven to 450°F. Place the pizza crust on a baking sheet.

Spread the goat cheese on top of the crust up to ½ inch from its edge. Drizzle the olive oil over the goat cheese; then scatter the herbs on top. Sprinkle evenly with the mozzarella.

Bake the pizza until the cheese is melted, about 10 minutes. Remove from the oven, transfer to a cutting board, and cut into slices.

Goat Cheese and Garlic with Extra-Virgin Olive Oil

MAKES 1 6-INCH PIZZA (*serves 1*) *or* 1 12-INCH PIZZA (*serves 4–6*)

This pizza offers a combination of pungent, irresistible flavors—garlic and goat cheese—happily married by the fruity flavor of good olive oil. If you'd like to moderate the taste of garlic somewhat, substitute roasted garlic (see Index), or use one of the garlic-flavored olive oils available in gourmet shops and well-stocked supermarkets. For that matter, try substituting any of the excellent flavored extra-virgin olive oils now available in such stores. A layer of thinly sliced sun-ripened tomatoes on top of or beneath the goat cheese makes a good addition. Or try oil-packed sun-dried tomatoes, cut into thin strips with kitchen scissors.

Prebaked pizza crust	*6-inch*	*12-inch*
Medium-sized garlic clove, peeled	*1*	*4*
Extra-virgin olive oil	*2 tablespoons*	*½ cup*
Fresh, creamy goat cheese, softened	*2 ounces*	*½ pound*
Shredded fontina cheese	*1 ounce*	*¼ pound*
Fresh basil, shredded fine	*½ tablespoon*	*2 tablespoons*

Preheat the oven to 450°F. Place the pizza crust on a baking sheet.

Press the garlic through a garlic press into a bowl. Add the oil and stir; then spread the mixture on top of the crust up to ½ inch from its edge. Spread the goat cheese on top of the garlic and oil. Sprinkle evenly with the fontina.

Bake the pizza until the cheese is melted, about 10 minutes. Remove from the oven, transfer to a cutting board, garnish with basil, and cut into slices.

Liptauer

MAKES 1 6-INCH PIZZA (*serves 1*) or 1 12-INCH PIZZA (*serves 4–6*)

A cheese spread popular in Eastern Europe, Liptauer makes a luscious and aromatic topping for prebaked pizza crusts. In its traditional form it is served cold and must be made at least a day in advance to give its flavors time to mellow. But baking the spread and serving it hot accomplishes the task in a matter of minutes. Feel free to adjust the seasonings to your own taste. If you like, mix in a little finely chopped anchovy fillet too.

Prebaked pizza crust	6-inch	12-inch
Cream cheese, softened	1 ounce	¼ pound
Fresh, creamy goat cheese, softened	1 ounce	¼ pound
Finely shredded sharp cheddar cheese	1 ounce	¼ pound
Fresh chives, chopped fine	½ tablespoon	2 tablespoons
Small capers, drained	1 teaspoon	4 teaspoons
Sweet paprika	½ teaspoon	2 teaspoons
Fresh parsley, chopped fine	½ teaspoon	2 teaspoons
Whole caraway seeds	⅛ teaspoon	½ teaspoon

Preheat the oven to 450°F. Place the pizza crust on a baking sheet.

In a bowl, mash together cheeses, herbs, and caraway seeds until they are well blended. Spread the cheese mixture on top of the crust up to ½ inch from its edge.

Bake the pizza until the cheese is melted and bubbly, about 10 minutes. Remove from the oven, transfer to a cutting board, and cut into slices.

Ricotta Soufflé

MAKES 1 6-INCH PIZZA *(serves 1)* or 1 12-INCH PIZZA *(serves 4–6)*

The charm of this pizza lies in the way its topping puffs up during the brief baking period. Serve it immediately for the best appreciation of its consistency. For a tangy alternative, substitute fresh, creamy goat cheese for half of the ricotta. You could also include a little finely chopped prosciutto in the mixture.

Prebaked pizza crust	*6-inch*	*12-inch*
Ricotta cheese, well drained	½ cup	2 cups
Grated Parmesan cheese	2 tablespoons	½ cup
Fresh parsley, chopped fine	½ teaspoon	2 teaspoons
Fresh chives, chopped fine	½ teaspoon	2 teaspoons
Salt and white pepper to taste		
Large egg, well beaten	1	4

Preheat the oven to 450°F. Place the pizza crust on a baking sheet.

In a mixing bowl, mash together the ricotta, Parmesan, parsley, chives, and salt and white pepper to taste. Add the egg and mix well.

Spread the ricotta mixture evenly over the surface of the pizza crust up to ½ inch from its edge.

Bake the pizza until the topping is puffed and golden, about 10 minutes. Remove from the oven, transfer to a cutting board, and cut into slices.

Baked Egg with Tomato and Pesto Sauces and Smoked Mozzarella

MAKES 1 6-INCH PIZZA *(serves 1)* or 1 12-INCH PIZZA *(serves 4–6)*

Serve this pizza as a sumptuous brunch dish. If you make the 12-inch version, carefully position one egg in each quarter of the pizza, cutting the finished pizza into four generous slices. Thin slivers of prosciutto or pieces of crumbled crisp bacon make a good addition; scatter them atop the eggs before you add the cheese. You can also make the pizza with one or the other of the sauces alone. If you can't find smoked mozzarella, substitute another good smoked cheese of your choice.

Prebaked pizza crust	6-inch	12-inch
Pizza sauce	1 ½ tablespoons	6 tablespoons
Pesto sauce	1 ½ tablespoons	6 tablespoons
Unsalted butter	1 tablespoon	¼ cup
Large egg	1	4
Smoked mozzarella cheese, shredded	2 ounces	½ pound
Fresh parsley, chopped fine	½ tablespoon	2 tablespoons

Preheat the oven to 450°F. Place the pizza crust on a baking sheet.

Spoon the two sauces into the center of the pizza crust and spread them over the surface up to ½ inch from the edge, swirling the sauces together but taking care not to blend them completely.

In a nonstick frying pan, melt the butter over medium-to-low heat. Carefully break the egg(s) in and fry, using the spoon to baste with the butter, until the white has set, about 1 minute. With a spatula, carefully transfer to the pizza. Sprinkle evenly with the smoked mozzarella.

Bake the pizza until the cheese is melted, about 10 minutes. Remove from the oven, transfer to a cutting board, garnish with fresh parsley, and cut into slices.

Scrambled Egg with Garlic-Herb Cream Cheese

MAKES 1 6-INCH PIZZA (*serves 1*) *or* 1 12-INCH PIZZA (*serves 4–6*)

I've often melted garlic-herb cream cheese—such as the popular Boursin brand—into scrambled eggs as I cook them. It made perfect sense to try the combination atop a pizza. Very thin slices of firm ripe tomato also go very well with this; you can layer them in between the cheese and the eggs. You can also add a layer of thinly sliced prosciutto, smoked ham, or smoked salmon; or substitute regular cream cheese or fresh creamy goat cheese for the garlic-herb variety. You might also want to try stirring a little freshly grated Parmesan cheese into the eggs as they cook.

Prebaked pizza crust	6-inch	12-inch
Garlic-herb cream cheese, softened	1½ ounces	6 ounces
Unsalted butter	1 tablespoon	¼ cup
Large egg, lightly beaten	1	4
Shredded mozzarella cheese	2 ounces	½ pound
Fresh chives, chopped fine	½ tablespoon	2 tablespoons

Preheat the oven to 450°F. Place the pizza crust on a baking sheet.

Spread the garlic-herb cream cheese on top of the crust up to ½ inch from its edge.

In a nonstick frying pan, melt the butter over medium-to-low heat. Add the beaten egg and cook, stirring occasionally, until it forms very soft, moist curds, 2 to 3 minutes; it should still be slightly liquid. With a spoon, distribute over the surface of the pizza. Sprinkle evenly with the mozzarella.

Bake the pizza until the cheese is melted, about 10 minutes. Remove from the oven, transfer to a cutting board, garnish with chives, and cut into slices.

Lox, Egg, and Onion

MAKES 1 6-INCH PIZZA *(serves 1)* or 1 12-INCH PIZZA *(serves 4–6)*

Rather than scrambling the lox with the eggs, as was done when making the delicatessen breakfast dish that inspired this recipe, I prefer to arrange thinly sliced smoked salmon on the base of the pizza and top it with the onion-flavored scrambled eggs. If you like, however, you can certainly do it the old-fashioned way, cutting the salmon into slivers and sautéing it along with the beaten egg.

Prebaked pizza crust	*6-inch*	*12-inch*
Cream cheese, softened	*1 ½ ounces*	*6 ounces*
Smoked salmon, sliced thin	*1 ounce*	*¼ pound*
Unsalted butter	*1 tablespoon*	*¼ cup*
Red onion, chopped fine	*2 tablespoons*	*½ cup*
Large egg, lightly beaten	*1*	*4*
Shredded fontina cheese	*2 ounces*	*½ pound*
Fresh chives, chopped fine	*½ tablespoon*	*2 tablespoons*

Preheat the oven to 450°F. Place the pizza crust on a baking sheet.

Spread the cream cheese on top of the crust up to ½ inch from its edge. Arrange the sliced salmon on top of the cream cheese.

In a nonstick frying pan, melt the butter over medium-to-low heat. Add the onion and sauté about 1 minute; then add the beaten egg and cook, stirring occasionally, until it forms very soft, moist curds, 2 to 3 minutes; it should still be slightly liquid. Spoon the mixture over the surface of the pizza. Sprinkle evenly with the fontina.

Bake the pizza until the cheese is melted, about 10 minutes. Remove from the oven, transfer to a cutting board, garnish with chives, and cut into slices.

Scrambled Egg and Bacon with Smoked Cheddar

MAKES 1 6-INCH PIZZA (*serves 1*) *or* 1 12-INCH PIZZA (*serves 4–6*)

Classic breakfast ingredients combine for a great morning pizza. Feel free to substitute smoked Gouda or any other smoked cheese you like for the cheddar; or use any nonsmoked cheese that melts well.

Prebaked pizza crust	6-inch	12-inch
Cream cheese, softened	1½ ounces	6 ounces
Smoked bacon	1 ounce	¼ pound
Unsalted butter	1 tablespoon	¼ cup
Large egg, lightly beaten	1	4
Shredded smoked cheddar cheese	2 ounces	½ pound
Fresh chives, chopped fine	½ tablespoon	2 tablespoons

Preheat the oven to 450°F. Place the pizza crust on a baking sheet.

Spread the cream cheese on top of the crust up to ½ inch from its edge.

In a nonstick frying pan, cook the bacon over medium heat until just crisp. Drain on paper towels.

Pour off all the fat from the frying pan and melt the butter over medium-to-low heat. Add the beaten egg and cook, stirring occasionally, until it forms very soft, moist curds, 2 to 3 minutes; it should still be slightly liquid. Spoon the mixture over the surface of the pizza. Crumble the bacon on top of the eggs and sprinkle evenly with the smoked cheddar.

Bake the pizza until the cheese is melted, about 10 minutes. Remove from the oven, transfer to a cutting board, garnish with chives, and cut into slices.

Scrambled Egg with Sun-Dried Tomatoes and Shaved Parmesan

MAKES 1 6-INCH PIZZA (*serves 1*) *or* 1 12-INCH PIZZA (*serves 4–6*)

Morning eggs take a decidedly Italian turn in this brunch pizza. If you'd like to make an even more aromatic version, use pesto sauce.

Prebaked pizza crust	6-inch	12-inch
Pizza sauce	3 tablespoons	¾ cup
Block Parmesan cheese	1½ ounces	6 ounces
Unsalted butter	1 tablespoon	¼ cup
Large egg, lightly beaten	1	4
Oil-packed sun-dried tomato, drained	2 pieces	8 pieces
Shredded mozzarella	2 ounces	½ pound
Fresh parsley, chopped fine	½ tablespoon	2 tablespoons

Preheat the oven to 450°F. Place the pizza crust on a baking sheet.

Spread the pizza sauce on top of the crust up to ½ inch from its edge. Using a cheese shaver or a swivel-bladed vegetable peeler, cut wide shavings of Parmesan and distribute them evenly on top of the sauce.

In a nonstick frying pan, melt the butter over medium-to-low heat. Add the beaten egg and cook, stirring occasionally, until it forms very soft, moist curds, 2 to 3 minutes; it should still be slightly liquid. Spoon the mixture over the surface of the pizza.

With a sharp knife or kitchen scissors, cut the sun-dried tomato pieces into thin strips and scatter them over the egg. Sprinkle evenly with the mozzarella.

Bake the pizza until the cheese is melted, about 10 minutes. Remove from the oven, transfer to a cutting board, garnish with parsley, and cut into slices.

Scrambled Egg Whites with Smoked Turkey and Light Cheeses

MAKES 1 6-INCH PIZZA *(serves 1) or* 1 12-INCH PIZZA *(serves 4–6)*

This is one of my favorite ways to enjoy familiar breakfast flavors and textures without an excess of fat. Seek out a well-stocked supermarket for the best selection of reduced-fat cheeses. If you like, substitute Canadian bacon—surprisingly low in fat—for the smoked turkey.

Prebaked pizza crust	6-inch	12-inch
Light cream cheese, softened	1½ ounces	6 ounces
Grated Romano cheese	½ tablespoon	2 tablespoons
Smoked turkey, sliced thin	1½ ounces	6 ounces
Butter-flavored nonstick cooking spray		
Large egg whites, lightly beaten	2	8
Shredded reduced-fat mozzarella or cheddar	2 ounces	½ pound
Fresh chives, chopped fine	½ tablespoon	2 tablespoons

Preheat the oven to 450°F. Place the pizza crust on a baking sheet.

Spread the light cream cheese on top of the crust up to ½ inch from its edge. Sprinkle evenly with the Romano cheese. Arrange the smoked turkey on top.

Heat a nonstick frying pan over medium-to-low heat. Remove from the heat, spray evenly with the nonstick cooking spray, and return to the heat. Add the beaten egg whites and cook, stirring occasionally, until they form very soft, moist curds, 2 to 3 minutes. Spoon the eggs over the surface of the pizza. Sprinkle evenly with the cheese.

Bake the pizza until the cheese is melted, about 10 minutes. Remove from the oven, transfer to a cutting board, garnish with chives, and cut into slices.

Index